CULTURES OF THE WORLD
Rwanda

Cavendish
Square

New York

Published in 2021 by Cavendish Square Publishing, LLC
243 5th Avenue, Suite 136, New York, NY 10016
Copyright © 2021 by Cavendish Square Publishing, LLC

Third Edition

Website: cavendishsq.com

This publication represents the opinions and views of the author based on his or her personal experience, knowledge, and research. The information in this book serves as a general guide only. The author and publisher have used their best efforts in preparing this book and disclaim liability rising directly or indirectly from the use and application of this book.

All websites were available and accurate when this book was sent to press.

Library of Congress Cataloging-in-Publication Data

Names: King, David C., author. | Morlock, Rachael, author.
Title: Rwanda / David C. King and Rachael Morlock.
Other titles: Cultures of the world (third edition)
Description: Third edition. | New York : Cavendish Square Publishing, 2021.
  | Series: Cultures of the world | Includes bibliographical references
  and index.
Identifiers: LCCN 2020057678 | ISBN 9781502662613 (library binding) | ISBN
  9781502662620 (ebook)
Subjects: LCSH: Rwanda--Juvenile literature.
Classification: LCC DT450.14 .K56 2021 | DDC 967.571--dc23
LC record available at https://lccn.loc.gov/2020057678

Writers: David C. King; Rachael Morlock, third edition
Editor, third edition: Rachael Morlock
Designer, third edition: Jessica Nevins
Picture Researcher, third edition: Jessica Nevins

Find us on

CONTENTS

RWANDA TODAY

RWANDA IS A COUNTRY OF INCREDIBLE NATURAL BEAUTY, populated by resilient people with ambitious goals. The tragic events of the 1994 Rwandan Genocide and the years of conflict leading up to it have cast a dark shadow over the nation's past. However, signs of growth and change are visible everywhere in Rwanda. Since the beginning of the 21st century, Rwanda has committed to a vigorous program of reconciliation and transformation.

ATTRACTIONS

Visitors to Rwanda are likely to be stunned by the diversity of the natural environment. Despite its small size, Rwanda contains tropical rain forests, sandy beaches, and sprawling grasslands broken up by volcanoes, lakes, and rivers. This hilly country seems to have a little of everything. Rwanda's biodiversity draws tourists, scientists, and nature lovers to four national parks where the wildlife is free to roam and where

Pangolins are among the 151 different mammal species that live in Rwanda.

native habitats explode with plant life. Primates fill the forests, while elephants, lions, rhinos, giraffes, and zebras graze and hunt in the southeastern savannas. Surprising creatures, like the pangolin, can also be found.

Beyond its natural wonders, Rwanda is also rich in cultural diversity. Colorful outdoor markets are a good place to get to know the people of Rwanda. Farmers and pastoralists sell their products, while artisans display a wide range of skilled crafts. Depending on the occasion, traditional songs and dances might enliven the market atmosphere.

DIVISIONS

All Rwandans today are known as one people—the Banyarwanda. This is a relatively recent development, since two main groups competed for power

and influence through most of Rwanda's history. The Hutu and the Tutsi lived side by side in Rwanda for at least five centuries. When European colonizers arrived in the country at the end of the 19th century, the competition became more heated. Colonizers reinforced and exaggerated differences between the Hutu and Tutsi, setting the stage for a destructive rivalry.

The tension boiled over in 1959 when a group of Hutu staged a revolution. The establishment of Rwanda as an independent state in 1962 only fueled the conflict further. From that time until the early 1990s, violence and discrimination between the groups prevented any real national growth. Still, the violence and hatred leading up to 1994 could hardly prepare the country for what happened next. The Rwandan Genocide was a coordinated effort to wipe out the Tutsi people and those viewed as sympathetic to them. It resulted in the killing of roughly 1 million people.

Even with its troubled past, Rwanda today is a place with great hope for the future.

The COVID-19 pandemic has stunted economic growth in Rwanda, but aggressive and creative policies have managed to minimize the health impacts.

BEGINNINGS

The horrors of the Rwandan Genocide seemed to be an impossible tragedy to overcome. Whether they were Hutu, Tutsi, or Twa, not a single Rwandan was left untouched by the violence and destruction that battered the land. However, as a Rwandan proverb says, "Ends and beginnings are identical." What seemed like an ending gave way to a wave of fervent reconciliation and peace that has been maintained for 25 years.

The country had to start over from a place of deep grief and poverty. With every year that passed, the situation for ordinary Rwandans seemed to marginally improve. Progress may have felt slow to those doing the hard work of rebuilding their country, but from the outside, it was clear that remarkable economic leaps were being made.

Today, Rwanda is well on its way to reaching its goals of becoming a middle-income country. The nation is thriving economically, fostering new industries, and offering a positive business environment to foreign and domestic entrepreneurs and investors. Rwanda is now considered to be one of best places to do business in Africa.

Beyond economic growth, signs of a healthy society are also evident in the thriving art world of Rwanda, the preservation of rich cultural heritage and traditions, the provision of universal health coverage, the representation of women in government, and the openness to new and creative solutions to old problems. It's undoubtable that Rwandans' impressive ability to work as one united people is responsible for its remarkable achievements. However, this progress comes amid concerns that Rwandan society is steadily becoming more repressive. The international community continues to keep a close eye on the country's leadership, while also applauding its movement toward a higher standard of living for its citizens.

GEOGRAPHY

The Virunga Mountains rise majestically in northwestern Rwanda. Their habitat supports a wide variety of plants and animals.

1

RWANDA'S IMPRESSIVE GEOGRAPHY is made up of rolling hills, dense mountain rain forests, volcanic mountains, and grasslands. The climate is surprisingly cool and comfortable for a country located so close to the equator. This temperate, mountainous climate has earned Rwanda a reputation as a "tropical Switzerland." The country's picturesque scenery includes sparkling lakes and rivers, volcanoes, and coffee and tea plantations.

More than 151 different mammals and 670 bird species call Rwanda home. Akagera National Park in the east is one of the few African parks where the "Big Five" species of leopards, lions, cape buffalo, elephants, and rhinoceros can all be found. Other native animals include giraffes, hippopotamuses, crocodiles, and aardvarks. Nearly hidden in the mists of the volcanic peaks are the magnificent mountain gorillas.

This small, landlocked nation, slightly smaller than the U.S. state of Maryland, is located in the very heart of Africa; it is 1,250 miles (2,000 km) east of the Atlantic Ocean and 880 miles (1,415 km) west of the Indian Ocean. With a population of roughly 12.7 million people, it has an estimated population density of 1,249 people per square mile (482 people per

Rwanda has a total area of 10,169 square miles (26,338 square kilometers).

Golden monkeys are among the many primate species found in Rwanda. This pair was spotted in Volcanoes National Park.

Rwanda is often called *le pays des mille collines* in French, which means "land of a thousand hills."

sq km). That makes Rwanda the second most densely populated country on the African continent.

On the west, Rwanda is bordered by the Democratic Republic of the Congo, on the north by Uganda, on the east by Tanzania, and on the south by Burundi.

LAND OF A THOUSAND HILLS

On a physical map of Africa, you can see a ridge that separates the Nile River basin, or watershed, from the basin of the Congo River. This ridge, which is part of the Great Rift Valley, cuts from north to south through western Rwanda at an average altitude of 9,000 feet (2,743 meters) above sea level. On the western edge of this ridge, the land slopes sharply to Lake Kivu and the Ruzizi Valley. The eastern edge drops more gradually, with rolling hills extending like waves across central plateaus. This hilly landscape is a distinctive feature of Rwanda's geography.

The entire landscape of rivers, high plateaus, and mountains is a product of Rwanda's position in the Great Rift Valley, which slices through Africa, from the Red Sea in the north to Mozambique in the south. The huge fault line that created the Great Rift Valley was formed when two of the earth's tectonic plates separated. As the plates pulled apart, large pieces of the earth's crust slid down between the plates. This resulted in the formation of escarpments (steep slopes or long cliffs) and ravines, often with dramatically steep sides. The western part of the Rift Valley, known as the Albertine Rift Valley, extends from Lake Albert in Uganda, through Rwanda, south to Lake Tanganyika, and beyond to Lake Malawi.

Earthquakes and volcanic eruptions along the fault line are not uncommon today, a sign that the plates are moving. If they keep moving apart, East Africa could separate from the rest of the continent in several million years.

REGIONS

Lake Kivu, the country's largest lake, and the Ruzizi River form Rwanda's western border with the Democratic Republic of the Congo. From this boundary on the edge of the Great Rift Valley, the land rises sharply to about 9,000 feet (2,743 m). The lake, with its jagged shoreline, has great mountain views and excellent beaches.

South of the lake region lies Nyungwe Forest, a large area of rain forest sprawled across mountains that stretch south to the border with Burundi. The forest is famous for its variety of plants and animals, including the black-and-white Angolan colobus monkey, which forms huge troops of up to 400. This is one of the oldest forest regions in Africa, making it a favorite area for scientific research.

North of Lake Kivu is the Virunga Range, a chain of eight volcanic mountains created by the same geologic pressure that produced the Great Rift Valley. The highest mountain, Mount Marisimbi, rises to an elevation of 14,787 feet (4,507 m).

Lake Kivu is famous for its beaches, peninsulas, and beautiful islands that form an archipelago.

The center of Rwanda is a series of plateaus with an average elevation of 5,600 feet (1,707 m) above sea level. This plateau region was once covered by forest, but most of the land has been cleared for farming, especially over the past century. Each plateau slopes from west to east and ends in an escarpment with marshland at the base. The capital, Kigali, is located in this plateau region.

Several small lakes in the central region have irregular borders created by the very steep hills surrounding them. Because of the pressing need for cropland, the slopes have been carefully terraced. Terrace crops include plantains, beans, and sweet potatoes. Most of this region is savanna grassland, with a few dense woods and scattered acacia thorn trees.

Only in the east do the hills and mountains give way to lower, flatter land. This is part of a huge lowland area called the Lake Victoria Basin. The Akagera River, with its many large papyrus swamps and small lakes, forms Rwanda's border with Tanzania. Much of the region is protected in the Akagera National

Rwanda's two rainy seasons bring heavy storms that can cause damaging flooding and landslides.

Park. The park is home to a great variety of plant and animal species.

WEATHER PATTERNS

Altitude is an important influence on climate, and Rwanda's highlands and mountains have a remarkably comfortable climate, despite being within a few degrees of the equator. In the Great Rift Valley in the west, the average annual temperature is 73 degrees Fahrenheit (23 degrees Celsius), and the average annual rainfall is about 30 inches (76 centimeters). In the mountains, the temperature decreases with altitude to an average of about 63°F (17°C), and rainfall increases to an average of 58 inches (147 cm). On the central plateaus, the temperature and rainfall averages are between those extremes. Temperatures in the capital city of Kigali hover around 70°F (21°C) throughout the year.

In terms of climate, Rwanda has four seasons: two wet and two dry. There is a short rainy season from October to December, followed by a short dry season in January and February. The long rainy season extends from March to May, and the long dry season lasts from June to September.

PLANT LIFE

The enormous variety of plant and animal species is divided into several unique ecosystems: Nyungwe Forest and the volcanic mountains of the west, the central highland grassland, and the lowlands of the east. The Nyungwe Forest National Park, for example, has at least 200 species of trees. The upper canopy of trees, reaching 200 feet (60 m), is dominated by slow-growing hardwoods such as African mahogany and Mulanje cedar. There is greater variety in the midstory canopy, and in the lower canopy, there are giant tree ferns and large lobelias. The forest also has more than 140 species of orchids. Begonias are represented among the 1,068 total plant species present in Nyungwe Forest.

AKAGERA NATIONAL PARK

In the years after Rwanda's civil war, Akagera National Park was suffering. Rwandans had fled their homes, and many sought safety in and around Akagera. Increased human activities degraded Akagera's plant and animal life. Native animals were either killed by poaching or forced out of their habitat. By 2002, native lions in Akagera were gone, and black rhinos disappeared by 2007.

As the country healed, the people of Rwanda prioritized protecting the environment. A 2009 contract with African Parks, a nonprofit organization, revitalized Akagera. New lions were introduced to the park in 2015, and black rhinos followed in 2017. Healthy populations of these animals are now thriving in Akagera, alongside hippos, cape buffalo, and other remarkable species. Part of this success comes from critical partnerships between conservationists and local communities. All Rwandans have a stake in protecting ecosystems, and conservation and tourism go hand in hand in supporting local communities.

Akagera National Park is a tropical savanna—the perfect habitat for giraffes, elephants, antelope, lions, and more.

The savanna grasslands of central Rwanda and parts of eastern Rwanda have scattered acacia thorn trees and euphorbia, which are cactus-like plants that have a milky sap and flowers without petals. Much of this central area is now used for growing crops and for pasture. Above about 6,500 feet (2,000 m), bamboo is dominant, especially in the Virunga Mountains.

The eastern region of Rwanda, warmer and wetter than the rest of the country, contains sprawling papyrus swamps that connect a series of small lakes. There are large areas of broad-leafed trees and smaller stands of acacia. Because it is isolated by mountains, several species of flowers, shrubs, and trees are endemic to (found only in) Akagera National Park.

ANIMAL LIFE

The various animal species living in Rwanda are found largely in the forest and savanna regions. A total of 151 mammal species live in the country. There are 670 known bird species in Rwanda. Today, national parks provide sanctuaries for wildlife native to Rwanda.

Poachers and warfare have taken a dramatic toll on Rwanda's wild areas. The populations of large animals, including elephants, lions, water buffalo, and giraffes fell dramatically at the turn of the 21st century. Some native populations disappeared entirely. Protected areas, such as Akagera National Park, lost up to two-thirds of their land. Fortunately, recent conservation efforts have made great strides in rebuilding national parks and protecting the habitat of native animals. Many species, including black rhinoceroses and lions, have been reintroduced to the parks.

Even with these setbacks, the variety of animal life is impressive. Akagera, for example, has 11 species of antelope, ranging from the eland, Africa's largest antelope, to the small common duiker. This park has a number of very rare species, such as the giant pangolin, a variety of anteater. The lakes support one of the largest populations of hippopotamus found anywhere in Africa, as well as large crocodiles. The grasslands in the east have small numbers of leopards, lions, and black rhinoceroses.

The forests and mountains of western Rwanda are most famous for their various primates. Nyungwe Forest National Park is home to 13 species, including the common chimpanzee and eight varieties of monkey. The colobus monkey is known for its acrobatics in the forest canopy. It is easily recognized by its black coloring and white whiskers, shoulders, and tip of tail. Other species include l'Hoest's monkey, a large primate with a gray and red coat contrasting with a white beard; the silver monkey; the rare owl-faced monkey; and the olive baboon.

The chimpanzees of Nyungwe are among the most popular tourist attractions in all of Rwanda. Visitors can take guided "chimpanzee treks" through the park, observing troops of about 30 to 60 animals. The chimpanzees are more closely related to humans than any other living creatures. They are known to use simple tools and, in captivity, have been taught to communicate with sign language.

The colobus monkey lives deep within Nyungwe Forest in troops with 200 to 400 monkeys.

The great study of chimpanzees, begun by Jane Goodall in 1960, continues today. While the research is centered in neighboring Tanzania, Rwanda has also been included in the study.

Nyungwe also has a variety of predators. Small numbers of leopards are still found in the forest, along with golden cats, wildcats, side-striped jackals, and three species of mongoose. Other mammals include the Congo clawless otter, giant forest hog, bush pig, and several types of squirrel. (The giant forest squirrel can glide from tree to tree, and the tree hyrax is a creature that looks like a guinea pig and has a bloodcurdling screech heard in many rain forest movies.)

Of all the animals in Rwanda, by far the most famous is the mountain gorilla. The largest of all primates, gorillas once lived in a wide swath of land in central Africa. For years, their numbers were diminished by poaching and human activities. Rwanda's mountain gorillas came dangerously close to extinction. Fortunately, conservation efforts have helped the number of wild gorillas increase. Today, there are more than 1,000 of the peaceful creatures living in their native African habitat. Over half of them live in Rwanda's Volcanoes National Park, with slightly smaller numbers living in Uganda and the Democratic Republic of the Congo.

Rwanda's mountain gorillas have received worldwide attention thanks to the research and conservation efforts of a number of scientists. Dian Fossey is one of the best-known scientists to study mountain gorillas in their native habitat. She studied and wrote about Rwanda's gorillas and urged immediate action in order to preserve and protect this species. Three years after Fossey's death in 1985, her efforts received worldwide publicity with the release of the film *Gorillas in the Mist*. The film helped to create great interest in protecting mountain gorillas and in gorilla tourism.

In the past few decades, guided treks to view mountain gorillas in their natural habitat have been a major source of tourism in Rwanda. Visitors must obtain a special permit to view gorillas on a trek through Volcanoes National Park. Revenue from these permits funds the conservation of gorilla habitats, fuels research, and supports local communities. Veterans of "gorilla

Grey crowned cranes are an endangered species in Rwanda. In traditional culture, they are a symbol of wealth and long life.

RWANDA'S MOUNTAIN GORILLAS

The magnificent mountain gorilla was unknown to the outside world until 1902, when a German explorer shot two. Over the next 50 years, studies showed that mountain gorillas were a species separate from the slightly smaller lowland gorillas. Efforts to protect them began in the 1920s with the formation of Albert National Park (now Virunga National Park).

In 1959, George Schaller started the first scientific study of how mountain gorillas live. Dian Fossey continued his work when she established the Karisoke Research Center in 1967. For nearly 20 years, she spent long periods in Volcanoes National Park, and her work made the world aware of the gorillas' nonaggressive behavior and sedentary, highly social life. Her efforts were a key reason that poaching was sharply curtailed. (The mountain gorilla population had dropped dramatically in the 1950s and 1960s.) Fossey was murdered in 1985, probably by the poachers she had struggled against for years.

Mountain gorillas live in groups headed by a male gorilla, called a silverback (*right*). There are 20 different gorilla families currently living in Volcanoes National Park.

treks" say there are few experiences more magical than an encounter with a mountain gorilla.

Mountain gorillas aren't the only remarkable species in Rwanda. Another impressive feature of Rwanda's wildlife is its variety of birds. The birds in western Rwanda are different from those in the eastern lowlands. The Nyungwe Forest is home to roughly 300 species, including at least 26 that are found only in this area of the Great Rift Valley. Some of the forest dwellers are known for their unusual colors, such as the great blue turaco, a large bird with bright blue, green, and yellow feathers. A few species are found only in this forest and the volcanic mountains, including the Kivu ground thrush, the red-faced woodland warbler, and the yellow-eyed black flycatcher.

The birdlife of eastern Rwanda features many species that are savanna dwellers, such as the lilac-breasted roller and the black-headed gonalek. In addition, a number of raptors, including hooded vultures and brown snake eagles, call this region home. Far more numerous are the water birds of the lakes and swamps. These include varieties of stork, crane, heron, egret, and shoebill.

Rwanda is also home to a wide variety of smaller creatures. There are well over 100 species of butterflies, as well as several kinds of large beetles and many varieties of ants, including the notorious army ant that marches through the forests in huge columns.

URBANIZATION

In the past, Rwanda has looked like a huge expanse of green from the air, with many small trees indicating tea, coffee, and banana plantations. Over time, this rural country has been changing. Fewer families depend on farms, and more Rwandans are migrating to cities. However, the majority of Rwandans still reside in rural areas, and 70 percent of citizens live by farming.

In the countryside, towns, villages, or clusters of houses are the main centers of activity. Houses are loosely clustered in family compounds, usually centered on a small hill. Each dwelling is encircled by an enclosure formed by a hedge, or palisade, of living plants. More enclosures extend to the rear of the dwelling owned by the head of the family. Livestock are also kept inside each family's enclosure.

Rwanda's cities are becoming larger and more populated. Kigali was a town of about 25,000 when it was chosen as the capital of the newly independent nation in 1962. It had the atmosphere of a small town and sprawled over several hills in the center of the country. Today, Kigali's population has mushroomed to more than 1 million people. Other cities have also bloomed. The World Bank and the Rwandan government have partnered on projects to support urbanization. Their goal is to build up Kigali and other cities with infrastructure that will support work and educational opportunities for city residents. Through these efforts, the cities of Muhanga, Rubavu, Nyagatare, Huye, Rusizi, and Musanze have grown as important urban centers in Rwanda.

Kigali is a booming city in central Rwanda. It is a cultural center that draws migrants in search of work, education, or cosmopolitan living.

INTERNET LINKS

gorillafund.org
Learn about the Dian Fossey Gorilla Fund, which continues Fossey's research and conservation efforts at the Karisoke Research Center and beyond.

www.nationalgeographic.com/travel/destinations/africa/rwanda/partner-content-rwanda-wildlife/
This slideshow from *National Geographic* presents a close-up view of Rwanda's impressive wildlife.

www.volcanoesnationalparkrwanda.com
Visit the website for Volcanoes National Park, the location of five of the eight Virunga Range volcanoes and the home of Rwanda's mountain gorillas.

HISTORY

This image of traditional Tutsi warriors is a testament to the country's long history, which is much more than just the story of its genocide.

2

ALL HUMAN HISTORY BEGINS IN Africa. The oldest hominid fossils on the continent date back 6 million years or more. Hominids are a scientific group that includes modern humans, the great apes, and their extinct ancestors. East Africa in particular has played a large role in hominid evolution. For this reason, East Africa and the Great Rift Valley are often called the cradle of humanity. Crucial evidence of ancient hominids has been found in Rwanda's eastern neighbor, Tanzania.

Homo habilis, one of the oldest species in the genus shared with *Homo sapiens* (humans) lived in Tanzania 2.4 million years ago.

New anthropological discoveries help fill in the constantly developing timeline of human ancestors and their movements around the world. The first migrations occurred within Africa. Later, some hominins ventured into Asia and then Europe. It is believed that *Homo sapiens* began migrating out of Africa roughly 200,000 years ago.

BUILDING THE KINGDOM

Settlement in present-day Rwanda likely dates back to 10,000 BCE. Ancient Rwandans were small in stature and lived by hunting and gathering. Descendants of these people, called the Twa, continue to make up a small

A replica of the king's palace at a museum in Nyanza brings traditional Rwandan architecture to life.

percentage of Rwanda's population today. Between the 5th and 11th centuries, Bantu-speaking farmers, known as the Hutu, discovered the region's fertile highlands. As they moved in, the Twa retreated from the best farmland and into the forests.

In the 14th century, another wave of migration brought pastoralists, or livestock raisers, into present-day Rwanda. These people, the Tutsi, soon gained dominance over the Hutu farmers. In the 15th century, Ruganzu Bwimba, a Tutsi leader, established a kingdom near Kigali. Each king, or *mwami*, after him tried to expand the kingdom. By the 19th century, Kigeri Rwabugiri, considered the country's greatest mwami, had expanded the kingdom almost to Rwanda's present borders.

Each king was the supreme authority and, in a magical way, was thought to embody Rwanda itself. Most kings appear to have been Tutsi. The king's authority was balanced, however, by a powerful queen and by a group called the *abiiru*, who had the task of making sure that royal decrees did not violate the kingdom's code of laws or morals. The abiiru could reverse an order of the king and also controlled the selection of a new king. This unusual system of checks and balances seemed to work well, and so did a form of federalism that allowed local chiefs, or kings, to govern small areas.

The deep division between the Hutu and Tutsi that led to later conflicts may have originated in Rwanda's unique version of feudalism, called *ubuhake*. This was a complex social and economic system. In the simplest terms, ubuhake allowed a subject to receive protection from a member of the higher class in exchange for services. This was not unlike feudalism in medieval Europe, in which peasants worked the land owned by nobles who kept the revenue in exchange for providing military protection. In Rwanda, the Tutsi cattle-raisers represented the wealthy, ruling class. They granted Hutu serfs the use of their land and cattle, but for a price.

Throughout the history of Rwanda's kingdoms, the country remained closed to the outside world. There was very little trade with other kingdoms, and there was no monetary system. Outsiders who tried to enter, such as the American explorer Henry Stanley in the 1870s, were greeted by a storm of arrows. Rwanda maintained that isolation until the arrival of Europeans in the 1890s.

GERMAN COLONIALISM

Throughout the second half of the 19th century, the colonizing powers of Europe engaged in a race to carve up Africa into colonies to be exploited for their resources. Germany, which did not become a unified nation until the 1870s, was a late entry in the race but quickly insisted on some share of colonies. At a meeting called the Berlin Conference held in 1885, Germany was allowed to claim Ruanda-Urundi (as Rwanda and Burundi were then called) as part of German East Africa, even though no European officials had ever set foot there.

From the German viewpoint, Tutsi cattle-raisers in the ubuhake system were like European nobles in terms of social and political structure. Europeans thought this class structure was based partly on physical differences: The Tutsi chiefs and nobles were very tall, especially in relation to the short, stocky Hutu farmers and the much smaller Twa. The Germans favored the Tutsi and backed their leadership roles. The Hutu did control small areas in the north until 1911 and 1912, when German troops helped the Tutsi overwhelm the region and incorporate it into the larger whole. The Hutu fought vigorously to hold on to their independence, and the bitterness between the cultural groups continued through the next half century and beyond.

The era of German power was brief and ended during World War I (1914—1918). The Germans ruled through the existing power structure of the region. Some of their largest impacts on the country came from allowing religious missions to set up bases. The missions, both Catholic and Protestant, established schools, medical centers, and farms.

Nyanza, located in southern Rwanda, was the kingdom's capital in the 19th century. This replica of the king's palace reminds visitors of the country's royal history.

The German colonial presence in Rwanda lasted from 1894 to 1918.

Local soldiers from German East Africa were called Askaris. They served the Germans during World War I.

BELGIAN COLONIALISM

While Germany was struggling for its survival during World War I, Belgium took control of Rwanda. This was partly in retaliation for Germany's invasion of neutral Belgium in 1914. In 1923, the League of Nations created Ruanda-Urundi as a League Mandate to be ruled by Belgium. The Belgians remained in control for about 40 years; after World War II (1939—1945), the League Mandate was replaced by a United Nations (UN) trusteeship in 1946.

Under Belgian rule, Rwanda kept a separate budget and administration, although in 1925, it was linked to the Belgian Congo. Within what was still called Ruanda-Urundi, each native kingdom remained pretty much independent, with its own sovereign and systems of justice, taxation, and administration.

ETHNIC IDENTITY

By the time Europeans arrived in Rwanda, the Tutsi, Hutu, and Twa were significantly integrated. They had lived together for centuries, clans were made up of members from multiple groups, and intermarriage was common. They shared language, culture, and religion.

In fact, Tutsi and Hutu classifications were primarily related to social class and the ubuhake system. The Tutsi were cattle-raisers, and the Hutu were farmers. However, there was social mobility within these groups. That meant that a Hutu farmer who grew wealthy enough to own cattle could become a Tutsi.

German and Belgian colonizers misunderstood this culture and applied European ideas to Rwanda. They looked for physical markers, like height and body shape, to divide Rwandans into ethnic groups. In the 1930s, the Belgians issued identity cards that assigned rigid ethnic categories. This fueled a harmful system of racialized difference and tensions.

Belgian rule was beneficial to Rwanda in material ways. Agricultural production was increased, and a good deal of money and effort went into the building of roads, schools, hospitals, and government buildings. However, in terms of human relationships, the Belgians managed to harden the lines between the Hutu and Tutsi. At first, the colonial rulers favored the elite Tutsi. However, Belgian leaders also wanted to make Rwanda more democratic. They encouraged Hutu leaders to participate in politics. By 1950, the Hutu, who formed a majority of the population, were demanding a greater voice in government and an end to Tutsi political domination. Throughout the 1950s, the Belgians gradually switched their support from the still-powerful Tutsi minority to the Hutu majority.

AN INDEPENDENT NATION

The winds of change were sweeping across Africa in the 1950s and 1960s. One colony after another demanded independence from Europe's colonial powers.

King Kigeli V (*front*) was the last monarch to rule Rwanda. After 1961, the king was exiled. He found a new home in the United States.

In Rwanda, the movement for independence was complicated by the growing tensions between the Hutu majority, determined to gain control of the country, and the Tutsi minority, which felt its power slipping away.

The first wave of violence erupted late in 1959, when a Hutu subchief was beaten by a group of Tutsi. Hutu gangs retaliated and rampaged through the country in what has been called the Hutu Revolution. Several hundred people were killed before Belgian authorities restored order. Like the Tutsi, the Belgians felt their power slipping away, and they turned to the UN for help. The UN refused to accept elections organized by the Hutu political party in 1960. New elections were held in 1961, but it was not until July 1962 that

Rwanda's independence was recognized, the monarchy was abolished, and a republic was formed, with Grégoire Kayibanda as president.

In spite of UN involvement and the creation of an independent nation, troubles and violence between the two ethnic groups continued. About 12,000 Tutsi were killed in December 1963 alone. Others fled. Between 1959 and 1964, about 150,000 Tutsi sought refuge in neighboring countries. The new government, controlled by the Hutu, set strict employment quotas to address the long-standing inequalities. The Tutsi were allowed only 9 percent of jobs, school positions, and government appointments, reflecting the fact that they made up only 9 percent of the population. Other steps were taken to reinforce Hutu supremacy. Kayibanda was reelected president in 1965 and again in 1969, but his administration became increasingly brutal and corrupt, causing even the Hutu to demand moderation.

Grégoire Kayibanda was the first president elected by independent Rwanda. Kayibanda founded the Hutu political party called PARMEHUTU.

In 1973, after the government drove practically all the Tutsi out of education establishments, Major General Juvénal Habyarimana led a military coup that drove Kayibanda from power. A period of relative calm followed. Since the Hutu now had a virtual monopoly on power, Habyarimana was easily reelected as president in 1978, 1983, and 1988. It soon became clear that Habyarimana's regime would continue to alienate the Tutsi. In addition, the steady decline in prices for Rwanda's products, especially tea and coffee, brought the economy close to collapse.

On October 1, 1990, a group of 7,000 Tutsi exiles, organized as the Rwandan Patriotic Front (RPF) and including some Hutu, launched an invasion from Uganda. The government received help from French, Belgian, and Zairean (now called Congolese) troops, and the uprising ended with a cease-fire. Thousands were imprisoned. Habyarimana promised reforms, but nothing happened. Instead, he strengthened the army and the army-trained militia

The rebel soldiers of the Rwandan Patriotic Front (*seen here*), were led by Major Paul Kagame. The force was largely made up of Rwandan Tutsi who had been living in exile in Uganda.

called Interahamwe ("those who fought together") and secured additional support from French troops.

The RPF, now headed by Major Paul Kagame, continued its raids and its training of new recruits. Kagame insisted that the goal was to restore democracy rather than to bring back the Tutsi into power.

As the violence continued, pressure from Western countries and the UN led to an agreement made at Arusha, Tanzania, in August 1993. The Arusha Agreement committed Habyarimana to reforms, including integration of the army with RPF troops. A transitional national assembly was to begin the reforms, supported by a UN force. The hope created by the agreement quickly vanished when extremists refused to accept it. By late 1993, the atmosphere in Rwanda was one of impending doom.

100 DAYS

In the spring of 1994, many Tutsi, including families of mixed Hutu-Tutsi marriages, began to flee the country. Government-controlled television and radio broadcast inflammatory messages denouncing the Tutsi as "the enemy." In a desperate bid for help, Habyarimana went to a conference of regional presidents. As he returned to Kigali on April 6, his jet plane was shot down by a surface-to-air missile. Both the Rwandan president and Cyprien Ntaryamira, the newly elected president of neighboring Burundi, died in the crash. Hours later, the killing began.

The well-planned violence against the Tutsi and any Hutu associated with them was led by the army commander Colonel Theoneste Bagosora. The goal was genocide—the killing of all the Tutsi. One of Bagosora's first acts was to order the killing of Prime Minister Agathe Uwilingiyimana, a Hutu "moderate." This was followed by the killing of 10 Belgian UN peacekeepers, which led Belgium to withdraw all its troops. Then, the way was open for the army and militia to launch "death squads" into Tutsi communities, killing, looting, and burning wherever they went.

The genocide claimed between 800,000 and 1,000,000 lives. At the start of the killing, there were more than 2,000 UN troops in Rwanda, but they made no attempt to stop the bloodshed. What went wrong?

UN soldiers had strict orders not to interfere. After 10 Belgian peacekeepers were killed, the UN force was reduced to 250. On April 30, the UN Security Council discussed the crisis for eight hours but carefully avoided using the word "genocide." If the killings were labeled genocide, the UN would have been obliged to "prevent and punish" those responsible, according to the provisions of the Genocide Convention that was written in response to the Holocaust. A decision in May to send 6,800 troops was delayed by debates over who would pay. By late August, the UN troops began to arrive, and most governments recognized that genocide had taken place.

Every day for the next three months, thousands of Tutsi and suspected Tutsi sympathizers were killed. Weapons ranged from sophisticated assault rifles to machetes and knives. Spurred on by radio and television, even women and children participated in the mass murder.

Within two days of the April 6 plane crash, the RPF launched a major offensive to stop the genocide. As they advanced, help from the UN did not come. The 2,165 UN troops in the country did not intervene because they were there as "monitors," not soldiers.

On July 4, the RPF captured Kigali, the capital. Now it was the turn of the Hutu to flee, mostly to Zaire (now called the Democratic Republic of the Congo). Two weeks later, the RPF announced that the war had been won, a cease-fire was declared, and a broad-based Government of National Unity was formed.

In April 1994, more than 8,000 Tutsi refugees fled to Niashishi in southern Rwanda to escape violence and seek the protection of French soldiers.

RECOVERY

Episodes of violence continued throughout the 1990s, and the roughly 2 million refugees crammed into camps in neighboring countries created a humanitarian

CHILDREN AND THE GENOCIDE

The genocide had a profound impact on the children of Rwanda. Young survivors saw their family members and neighbors killed and injured, or came close to death themselves. The UN estimates that 300,000 children died. Another 95,000 were orphaned. Many of the children who had lost family members or been separated from their parents ended up in orphanages or with foster families. Many older children became the primary caregivers for their younger siblings and other orphans. In some cases, children were born as the result of the widespread acts of sexual assault that occurred during the genocide.

Many children and adults have suffered from post-traumatic stress disorder (PTSD) and other mental health issues as a result of witnessing violence and death during the genocide. Even decades later, the trauma of the genocide affects the survivors.

> "We are prepared that what happened here should never happen again, not only in Rwanda, but anywhere in the world."
> —President Paul Kagame, April 2004

crisis. Lack of food, clean water, and sanitary facilities led to disease, including a cholera epidemic at one camp that resulted in thousands of deaths.

The Government of National Unity, with Pasteur Bizimungu as president, took control in July 1994. Major General Paul Kagame was appointed defense minister and vice president. Over the next few years, Kagame emerged as the real power in Rwanda. In March 2000, Bizimungu resigned, and Kagame was sworn in as president. He continued Rwanda's efforts to restore peace and stability and to end the ethnic strife.

In November 1994, the UN Security Council set up the International Criminal Tribunal for Rwanda (ICTR) to try those accused of genocide. By 1996, the year UN troops left Rwanda, the first suspects were on trial. In June 2002, however, there were still 115,000 genocide suspects in prison camps. To get the wheels of justice to turn more swiftly, the *gacaca* (ga-CHA-cha) judicial system was started to review lesser crimes for those accused of participating in the 1994 genocide.

Gacaca was launched on June 18, 2002, and trials began in February 2005. This local court system was modeled after a traditional justice system that used community hearings to resolve local disputes. Gacaca was enacted at the village level. More than 250,000 judges, men and women elected by their own communities on the basis of their integrity, presided at hearings of prison detainees accused of genocide-related crimes. The system worked by bringing the detainee back to the scene of the alleged crime. Local residents who witnessed the events were called upon to accuse or defend the person in an attempt to get at the truth of what happened.

From 2005 to 2012, up to 11,000 gacaca courts operated in Rwanda.

Gacaca was developed as part of a restorative justice system. The hope was to achieve unity and reconciliation in the country through justice. The court system corresponded with other efforts aimed at healing. In 2003, President Paul Kagame ordered the release of detainees who had already served time equal to the sentences they would have received if convicted. More than 22,000 prisoners were released in 2003 and another 4,500 in 2004. An additional 36,000 were freed to participate in gacaca hearings in July 2005. Prisoners also received one month of training at solidarity camps, where they learned about Rwandan history, reconciliation, and justice.

The gacaca courts completed their mission and were closed in 2012. About 65 percent of the trials ended in guilty verdicts. A few years later in 2015, the UN-led ICTR finished its work. ICTR's trials for higher crimes resulted in the indictment of 93 individuals.

LOOKING AHEAD

Rwanda engaged in a period of rapid rebuilding following the genocide. The international community, undoubtedly moved by a sense of guilt for their inaction during the genocide, responded with many forms of assistance and investment. However, there is no denying that serious problems remain. Besides internal challenges within Rwanda, the genocide and its aftermath have led to international tensions.

After the RPF victory, over 1 million Hutu refugees found protection in the Democratic Republic of the Congo (DRC), then called Zaire. About 850,000 settled in refugee camps near the city of Goma. Although some were merely citizens in fear for their lives, the refugees also included those who had masterminded and facilitated the genocide. These criminals used refugee camps as training grounds for extremist Hutu forces. Though many Hutu fighters eventually returned to Rwanda and attended solidarity camps, others continued their attacks among the refugees.

Rwanda was deeply entangled in the uprisings and upheaval of the DRC from 1993 to 2003. The UN has reported that Rwanda took part in human rights abuses by killing Hutu refugees living in the DRC. Rwanda is said to have carried out these attacks while backing the revolution that placed Laurent Kabila in power in 1997. The UN also reports that Rwanda helped insurgent forces in the DRC, but the government of Rwanda continues to deny these charges. In 2012, the United States, the United Kingdom, and the Netherlands all suspended their aid to Rwanda as a result of such allegations.

Rwanda has also had a difficult relationship with France. Tensions were especially high after the genocide, when the French alliance with the Hutu government was scrutinized. President Kagame has accused the French of helping Hutu extremists escape from Rwanda. In turn, the French government has held Kagame responsible for the missile that killed President Habyarimana. In response, Kagame suspended all diplomatic ties with France from 2006 to 2009. Kagame also launched an investigation into the attack on Habyarimana's plane. The 2010 findings indicated that the attack was launched by Hutu extremist soldiers in order to spark anti-Tutsi action.

Despite tensions with the DRC and France, Rwanda has managed to forge important alliances with other nations. In 2009, Rwanda became the 54th country to join the Commonwealth. Traditionally, this union of nations had a shared history of being previously colonized by Great Britain. Rwanda became only the second country, after Mozambique, to join the Commonwealth without historical ties to Great Britain. Rwanda has also maintained its membership in the African Union (previously known as the Organization of African Unity) since 1963.

Beyond foreign relations, Rwanda has had to navigate its new identity as a country. In 2001, new national symbols were created to reflect the story and future of Rwanda. A flag, anthem, and coat of arms were introduced as signs of hope, change, and unity. Restructuring in the government has also led to important constitutional changes. In 2003, Kagame won the first presidential election Rwanda had held since the genocide. He was reelected in 2010 and 2017.

Under Kagame, Rwanda appears to be flourishing. The country has made rapid economic progress since the 100 days of terror in 1994. One of the greatest successes of Rwanda's rebuilding has been the reduction of ethnic tension through reconciliation. This spirit of building unity helped persuade an estimated 2 million refugees to return to Rwanda. Identity cards, listing each Rwandan as Hutu, Tutsi, or Twa, have been discarded. With strict laws outlawing divisionism and talk of ethnicities, however, some fear that peace has been maintained at the cost of personal freedoms. There are troubling signs that the firm grip of the government under President Kagame has become repressive.

The Kigali Genocide Memorial was inaugurated in April 2004. The memorial contains tombs with the remains of 250,000 genocide victims.

INTERNET LINKS

kgm.rw
Visit the website of the Kigali Genocide Memorial, which strives to help visitors remember and learn from the past while honoring genocide victims.

neveragainrwanda.org
Never Again is a nongovernmental organization in Rwanda that works to promote peace and healing through education and community-building, especially among young people.

www.newtimes.co.rw/section/read/30993
This article explores some of the museums dedicated to uncovering and commemorating Rwanda's history beyond the genocide.

www.pbs.org/wgbh/pages/frontline/shows/rwanda/etc/cron.html
PBS provides a detailed timeline of the genocide in Rwanda.

GOVERNMENT

President Kagame, seen here on a billboard in Kigali, has become a central figure in Rwanda's story in the years since the genocide.

3

T HE REPUBLIC OF RWANDA TODAY provides a model of government in some ways. Recent changes to the constitution have been aimed at more fairly representing Rwanda's multiethnic and diverse population. Most notably, Rwanda has the highest percentage of women lawmakers in the world. With women filling 61 percent of legislative roles, Rwanda is far ahead of most other countries. For example, in the United States in 2020, women made up only 23 percent of Congress. However, Rwanda's advances have been made over the course of a long and troubled history.

"The founding principle of the Republic of Rwanda is: 'Government of Rwandans, by Rwandans and for Rwandans.'"
—The Constitution of Rwanda

ESTABLISHING THE REPUBLIC

The basic problem Rwanda faced after gaining independence on July 1, 1962, was finding a way to resolve the conflict between the two largest ethnic groups: the Hutu and the Tutsi. Government was one arena in which the two could try to find peaceful resolutions to their differences. Instead, each group tried to gain control of the government in order to dominate the other. For the first three decades after independence, government activity reflected the Hutu majority's resolve to gain power.

The constitution adopted on November 24, 1962, established a presidential republic based on direct elections and universal adult suffrage (the right to vote). The president was the head of state and appointed a cabinet of ministers to head various departments. Both the president and a National Assembly could introduce legislation. There was also an independent judiciary. This first constitution was written primarily by Belgian colonists with little participation from the Rwandans whose rights and powers were being determined.

Grégoire Kayibanda was the first president of the new republic. He was a former teacher and a journalist for a Catholic newspaper. He was also the founder of a political party—PARMEHUTU (Party for the Emancipation of the Hutu People). Supported by the Hutu majority, he was reelected in 1965 and 1969. Although on paper the Rwandan constitution called for a multiparty system and the protection of human rights, the lived experience of Rwandans was quite different.

HUTU EXTREMISM

Extremist elements among the Hutu were not satisfied with Kayibanda. In July 1973, two months before the next election in which Kayibanda was to be the only candidate, the government was overthrown by the national guard, led by its commander, Major General Juvénal Habyarimana. The National Assembly of lawmakers was dissolved, all political activity was outlawed, and Habyarimana was made the head of the government.

Over the next 20 years, the Tutsi people, who had once dominated Rwanda, became an oppressed minority. Because thousands fled to neighboring countries, the remaining Tutsi made up only 9 percent of the population. They were now subject to strict quotas, such as being allowed no more than 9 percent of school positions and government appointments.

In 1975, Habyarimana's government formed a political party, the National Revolutionary Movement for Development (MRND). Under a new constitution approved in 1978, this was the only legal party. Habyarimana combined the power of the main leadership roles of head of state and head of government under the presidency. He was elected president under this new constitution and was reelected in 1983 and 1988.

During this period of Hutu dominance, nothing was done to resolve the basic ethnic conflict. Tutsi refugees launched border raids, but these were easily quashed. During the same period, a split developed among the Hutu, and the army came to be controlled by northerners eager to weaken the Tutsi minority even further. However, when the new Rwandan Patriotic Front (RPF) invaded from Uganda in 1990 and 1991, Habyarimana was forced to revise the constitution to allow for other political parties, and he appointed some members of opposition parties to cabinet posts. This was a step toward a joint Hutu-Tutsi government, but the RPF wanted more.

GOVERNMENT IN CRISIS

Following more violence between 1991 and 1993, a peace agreement was signed at Arusha, Tanzania, in August 1993. Both sides were to share power in a transitional government, and the army was to be integrated. After months of delay, Habyarimana was installed as president in January 1994, but then was killed soon after when his plane was shot down.

The genocide followed, with the extremist Hutu soldiers and militia determined to destroy the Tutsi people. When the violence was finally ended by the RPF, more than one-fourth of Rwanda's population had fled or been killed.

REDEFINING RWANDA

When the RPF took over in July 1994, the movement's leaders named two Hutu moderates to a transition government that would lead the country out of crisis. Pasteur Bizimungu was named president, and Faustin Twagiramungu was appointed prime minister. Paul Kagame, leader of the RPF, became vice president. There were still roughly 2 million refugees, but these were now Hutu who feared that the RPF would seek revenge. Over the next five years, however, the government and the people worked hard at reconciliation, and by 2000, nearly all the Hutu refugees had returned.

Rwanda's national military is called the Rwanda Defense Force (RDF). Most troops are part of the army, but the RDF also includes a small air force and paramilitary units. Soldiers and airmen are volunteers. In 2019, there were about 32,000 soldiers in the army and 500 air force members. The RDF has taken part in international missions on behalf of the African Union and the UN Peacekeeping Forces.

Rwanda's commitment to preventing genocide worldwide led to the RDF's engagement in the Darfur region of Sudan. Rwanda was the first country to respond with military action to protect civilians when reports of genocide in Darfur reached the international community. Rwandan soldiers have been present in the region since 2004, and they are still one of the largest groups of peacekeepers in the area.

Rwanda has committed to preventing genocide around the world. President Kagame is seen here at the 2019 "Walk to Remember," alongside the Belgian and Ethiopian prime ministers.

After President Bizimungu and Prime Minister Twagiramungu resigned in 2000, Paul Kagame became the nation's fifth president. A new constitution was approved in 2003, and in August the transition government was dissolved. Kagame was elected president in the first elections since the genocide. A month later, elections for the legislature were held.

In the years that have followed, some observers have questioned the government's commitment to full equality for all cultural groups. They also argue that too much power is being concentrated in Kigali, with very little self-government being allowed in the local communities. There is evidence that the government is allowing less and less political dissent. Many outsiders were especially alarmed by the arrest, trial, and conviction of Pasteur Bizimungu.

In early 2004, foreign observers were shocked to learn that Bizimungu had been arrested and put on trial. A few weeks later, Bizimungu was found guilty and sentenced to a prison term of 15 years for civil disobedience, associating with criminal elements, and embezzlement of state funds.

President Kagame was the first Tutsi to be elected president since Rwandan independence. Under his leadership, ethnic divisions have been outlawed.

Amnesty International immediately denounced the trials as a violation of Rwanda's constitution and criminal justice system in order to repress political opposition. "Through these actions," Amnesty International declared, "the Rwandese government is closing the door to any form of free and open political debate and discussion." Defense attorneys insisted that the defendant was not guilty of any of the accusations.

The Rwandan government was equally insistent that the trials were fair and necessary; however, President Kagame granted a pardon to Bizimungu three years into his sentence. Officials say that the Commission for National Unity and Reconciliation continues to monitor the activities of individuals and groups that may try to undermine Rwanda's policy of unity and reconciliation.

PRESIDENT KAGAME

President Kagame held onto his office through elections in 2003 and 2010. He won the 2010 election with 93 percent of the vote. As the end of his second term approached, something unusual happened. The 2003 constitution stipulated that the presidency was a seven-year term with the opportunity for one

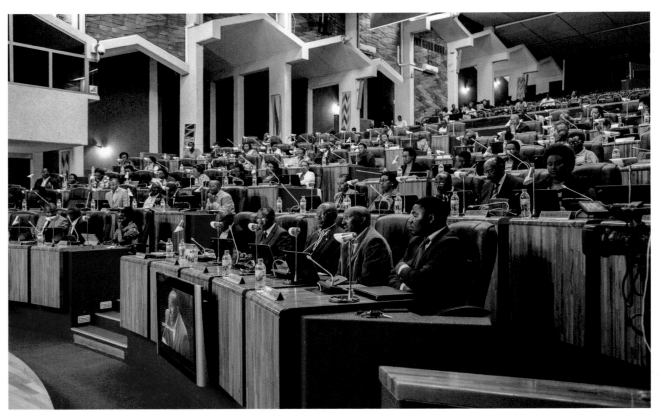

In 2015, Parliament discussed constitutional amendments that would allow Kagame to run again in 2017.

reelection. However, momentum grew within Parliament to amend this part of the constitution. A referendum pushing for constitutional changes led to a parliamentary vote in 2015. It passed in both houses with 98 percent of the vote. The resulting constitutional amendments reset the limitations on presidential terms. They also shortened the presidential term from seven to five years. These new term limits will take effect with the election of 2024.

As a result of the 2015 constitutional amendments, President Kagame was free to run for another term in 2017, as well as in the future presidential elections of 2024 and 2029. Kagame viewed the constitutional change as a call for his continued service as president. He successfully won reelection in 2017 with 98 percent of the vote. It is now possible for Kagame to remain in power until 2034. This extension of Kagame's leadership is concerning for those who fear that he is becoming increasingly authoritarian. Intimidation, bans, and violence against journalists and members of opposition parties, especially surrounding the 2010 and 2017 presidential elections, have raised red flags for international observers.

GOVERNMENT STRUCTURE

Rwanda's constitution guarantees the basic civil rights of all citizens; bans the existence of political parties based on race, religion, or ethnic background; and expresses Rwanda's determination to eliminate ethnic conflict by outlawing divisionism and genocidal ideology. Although political parties cannot be organized along ethnic lines, the government is designed to support a multiparty system. The major political parties today are the Rwandan Patriotic Front, the Social Democratic Party, and the Liberal Party.

President Paul Kagame and First Lady Jeannette Nyiramongi Kagame pay their respects at the Kigali Genocide Memorial in 2019.

"I attribute our constant social and economic progress to the broad and deep involvement of women in our affairs."
—President Kagame, 2015

The three branches of government—executive, legislative, and judicial—are based on models from Western Europe and the United States.

In the executive branch, the president is the head of state and is elected to a five-year term, starting in 2024. Presidential elections are determined by universal suffrage (all citizens age 18 and over are allowed to vote). The president appoints a cabinet and a prime minister to oversee the carrying out, or execution, of national laws and policies.

The legislative branch is Parliament, which consists of two chambers: a Chamber of Deputies and a Senate. There 80 members of the Chamber of Deputies. Among these are 53 elected members, 24 women chosen by provincial councils, 2 members chosen by the National Youth Council, and 1 member chosen by by the Association of the Disabled. All deputies serve five-year terms. The 26 members of the Senate serve eight-year terms. Local councils elect 12 senators, 8 are appointed by the president, 1 is selected from a public university, another is selected from a private university, and four are chosen by the Forum of Political Organization. At least 30 percent of the senators must be women. Most new pieces of legislation

According to Rwanda's constitution, at least 24 out of 80 deputies in the Chamber of Deputies must be women. However, women can also be elected to the remaining, unreserved seats. That's what happened in 2008 when Rwanda far surpassed its gender quota. As a result of the election, 56 percent of deputies were women. At that time, Rwanda was the first and only country in the world to have a legislative body with the majority of seats filled by women.

In the most recent election of deputies in 2018, 49 women were elected, representing 61 percent of the Chamber. In 2019, 10 women were elected to the Senate, making up 38 percent of the total of 26 seats. Women currently make up half of the cabinet ministers and Supreme Court justices. Rwanda continues to lead the world when it comes to women's representation in government.

Citizens in Rwanda participated in the parliamentary elections of 2018. They voted to fill 53 of the 80 seats in the Chamber of Deputies.

have to be passed by both chambers and then are signed into law by the president.

Rwanda's judicial system is modeled on the Belgian code of law combined with local laws and traditions. The highest court is the Supreme Court, consisting of 14 judges appointed for life by the Senate. The High Court of the Republic is below the Supreme Court, and both can hear appeals from local courts. A separate court in each local governmental unit considers both criminal and civil cases.

Voter turnout for parliamentary and presidential elections is exceptionally high, but critics worry that Rwanda does not have a healthy, multiparty system.

Previously, the nation was divided into 12 prefectures. That changed in 2006 when the prefectures were replaced by five provinces. These include the Northern, Eastern, Southern, and Western provinces. The city of Kigali is the fifth province. Redefining provinces was an effort to equalize the distribution of power throughout Rwanda and prevent the formation of dominant ethnic and political units.

INTERNET LINKS

www.britannica.com/biography/Paul-Kagame
Read the *Encyclopedia Britannica* entry on Paul Kagame for more insight into Rwanda's long-term president.

www.gov.rw
The official website of the government of Rwanda provides basic information about the government structure and links to more in-depth news and resources.

www.parliament.gov.rw/index.php?id=2
The Rwandan Parliament website updates regularly with information about legislation and lawmakers in Rwanda.

As of 2020, Rwanda, Cuba, and Bolivia were the only countries in the world with more women than men in their legislative branches.

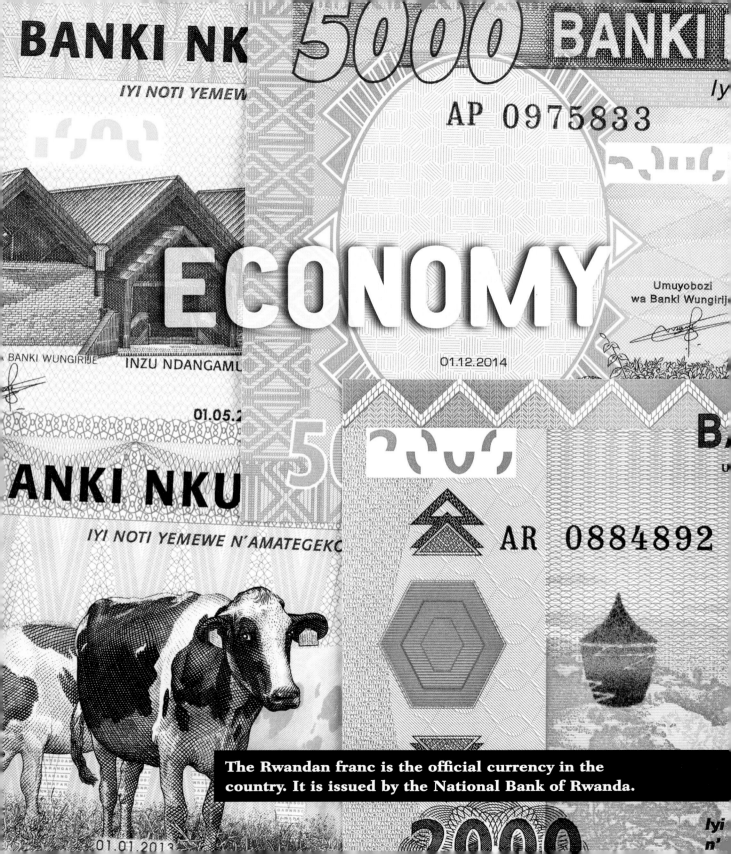

The Rwandan franc is the official currency in the country. It is issued by the National Bank of Rwanda.

RWANDA HAS OVERCOME INCREDIBLE challenges in the years since the genocide. The widescale deaths and damage to infrastructure nearly destroyed Rwanda's economy. Over the years, Rwanda not only regained its pre-conflict status, it also made significant improvements.

With a set of long-term development goals called Vision 2020, Rwanda attempted a dramatic economic overhaul between 2000 and 2020. The goal was to transform Rwanda from a poor country reliant on subsistence agriculture to a thriving, service-based economy. Rwanda did not reach its goal of becoming a middle-income country in 2020, but it has reset its program with the aim to be middle income by 2035 and high income by 2050. The country will keep moving forward with a new set of economic goals called Vision 2050.

In many ways, Rwanda is a struggling nation. As one of the most crowded countries in Africa, it still relies heavily on agriculture to feed its growing population. Rwanda has little industry, few mineral resources, and an outdated transportation system. After the genocide, a large number of people were widowed or orphaned, and thousands of Rwandans still suffer physical and psychological hardships because of the tragedy.

These negative factors are huge, but Rwanda has a number of valuable assets. The spectacular natural beauty of the country is one of those assets, including its primates, especially the famous mountain gorillas. The scenery and the wildlife have made tourism a major source of badly

Vision 2020 was designed to raise Rwanda's standard of living. Markers such as life expectancy, maternal and child mortality rates, poverty levels, economic growth, and educational enrollment have been used to measure the country's progress. They are among 48 different indicators that were tracked. Vision 2020 was ambitious, and many of its specific goals have not yet been reached. Some of Rwanda's significant improvements are recorded in the chart below.

Indicators	2000	2020 estimates	Vision 2020 Goal
GDP per capita	$220	$820	$1,240
Population living below the national poverty line	60 percent	39 percent	20 percent
Life Expectancy	49 years	69 years	66 years
Infant Mortality (deaths per 1,000 births)	107	26	27
Maternal Deaths (per 100,000 births)	1,071	210	200
Population with access to clean water	52 percent	57 percent	100 percent
Population with access to electricity	2 percent	53 percent	75 percent
Literacy rate	48 percent	73 percent	100 percent

needed foreign income. The environment is one of Rwanda's greatest resources in its attempts to build a more prosperous economy.

Another great asset is the people. Since the nightmare of the mid-1990s, the Rwandan people have displayed remarkable courage, determination, and skill. They have rebuilt their ravaged population and worked to end ethnic hatred.

AGRICULTURAL IMPROVEMENTS

The number of people engaged in farming in Rwanda has decreased in the 21st century. However, it is still the main source of income and livelihood for about 70 percent of Rwanda's population. Most of the farming is subsistence agriculture, which means that a family produces enough to meet its own needs, with little or nothing left over to sell for profit.

Because the country is so crowded, every available acre has to be producing food, even in the best of times. The genocide, however, left thousands of widows, many with young children, struggling to keep their family farms functioning. Those who could not manage slid into poverty. By 2000, about 60 percent of Rwanda's people lived below the national poverty line.

A farm family has to work hard on its small plot through two growing seasons, the first from September to January or February, the second from March to August. The main tools of Rwandan farmers are machetes, hoes, and a lot of dedicated labor. Very few farmers in the country use pesticides or fertilizers. Farmers grow a wide variety of crops, including corn, bananas, beans, sorghum, potatoes, plantains, and cassava. Some foods, like beans, sorghum, and corn, are harvested at specific times, while the other main crops can be grown year-round.

Agriculture accounts for 63 percent of Rwanda's earnings from exports. Farmers are also encouraged to grow one of Rwanda's important cash crops, either coffee, tea, tobacco, or chrysanthemums. The flowers are used in the production of an insecticide called pyrethrum, which is an important source of foreign income. Pyrethrum is mainly exported to Europe.

Coffee is Rwanda's primary export. It is grown on small farms, cooperatives, and plantations. While coffee has been an important cash crop since the colonial period, production fell 37 percent between 1990 and 2002. This decline was caused more by a drop in world prices rather than by the genocide. New programs and foreign assistance worked to reverse that decline, and since then Rwanda has had an advantage in the world coffee market: The soil, hilly terrain, and cool climate produce exceptional coffee beans.

The country's farm families have steadily increased the number of livestock animals since 2001. Cattle, sheep, and goats graze on open land and are kept

About 46 percent of the land in Rwanda is arable, or fit for growing crops. Terrace farming is one way of maximizing the available land.

"Rwandan coffee has a nutty, fruity flavor you can't find anywhere else in the world."
—David Griswold, coffee importer

Cows have been culturally and economically important in Rwanda since pre-colonial days.

in family compounds at night. In fact, the smaller ruminants (grazing animals), especially goats, are proving increasingly popular. Pigs and rabbits are also common livestock in rural areas. In 2018, there were about 1.16 million heads of cattle in the country, and milk production was measured at 899,000 tons (816,000 metric tonnes).

Even with the majority of the population engaged in farming, Rwanda does not make enough food to sustain itself. Food from other countries makes up a large percentage of Rwanda's imports. Over time, the government hopes to reduce the number of people engaged in agriculture to 50 percent and embrace a service economy instead. In the meantime, programs are underway to make agriculture more efficient and sustainable.

RESOURCES AND INDUSTRIES

Industries provide roughly 17 percent of the country's income, or gross domestic product (GDP), but their potential for growth is limited. Most manufacturing involves making products for local consumption, such as beverages, soap, furniture, shoes, a few plastic products, cement, cigarettes, and textiles. About 6 percent of Rwanda's labor force worked in industry in 2017.

Although industry is growing, it is difficult to export products to other countries for income. For one thing, the country lacks the infrastructure for industrial expansion. For example, there are only 7,450 miles (11,989 km) of roads in the entire country, and less than a quarter of those miles are paved. Also, Rwanda has no railroads, although the roads do provide a link to the Uganda-Kenya railroad. One way Rwanda can trade with distant lands is through Kenya's port of Mombasa, but getting products there is a cumbersome and expensive journey. Foreign investors are more interested in commercial ventures, like financing facilities for tourism.

Mineral production contributes even less to the economy. Practically all the nation's mines were closed during the genocide. Since 1995, there has been a gradual reopening of some mines. Tin and tungsten are the primary resources, but modest exports of tantalite, columbite, gold, and beryl are also managed.

SMALL ENTERPRISES

Rwandan handicrafts offer one of Rwanda's best hopes for modest economic growth. Different groups have preserved traditional crafts, including making pottery, carving wood, and weaving baskets, mats, and wall hangings. Some also show great skill making musical instruments, beadwork, and jewelry. If tourism continues to grow, sales of local items should increase.

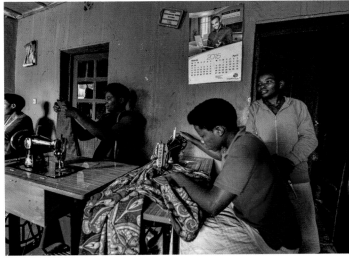

Textiles are among the products made in Rwanda. The seamstresses pictured here work at the Tyazo Market in Tyazo, Kirambo.

In 2018, the Ministry of Trade and Industry launched a new program called Made in Rwanda (MIR). This initiative increases access to raw materials and encourages people to produce, sell, and buy goods within Rwanda. As the government urges a movement away from agricultural activities, it hopes to expand industry, especially in the private sector. An annual MIR exposition allows vendors to show off their locally made products to the public and broaden their market. This is one way the government has tried to balance trade so that imports do not outweigh exports so dramatically.

FISHING

Fishing has been a small but valuable industry for many years, operated by local cooperatives (groups of several fisher families). There are 24 lakes in Rwanda, but most fishing takes place in lakes Kivu, Muhazi, and Mugasera. The most popular fish species caught in lakes are sambaza, Nile tilapia, and African catfish. Fish farmers also raise tilapia and catfish within cages in the lakes or in ponds.

Methane gas from Lake Kivu is a natural resource for producing nitrogen fertilizer and fuel.

During the genocide and for several years after, the lakes were not adequately restocked, so the output declined steadily. Since then, growing support for fish farms has helped to revive the industry. Fishing is still dominated by family farms and small-holder fishers. Since businesses cannot meet the demand for

Some international organizations sponsor artisan-based enterprises in Rwanda. For example, in 2019, the Lemonaid and ChariTea Foundation from Germany began promoting a ceramic cooperative among the Batwa (the Twa's name for themselves) through the African Initiative for Mankind Progress Organization (AIMPO). The Batwa have a long history of pottery production, but they have fallen on hard times as a result of their marginalized status and the degradation of their traditional forest homeland. The project aims to help the Batwa expand their educational and training opportunities, commit resources to their craft, and develop new, competitive marketing strategies.

Sambaza are a specialty fingerling caught by Lake Kivu fishers. These sardine-like fish are sold at markets and in restaurants.

fish within Rwanda, it is also imported, mainly from Uganda and Tanzania.

TRADE

Even though nearly three-fourths of the people are engaged in farming, Rwanda still has to import some food products. In addition, the country needs to buy a wide variety of products from other countries, including machinery, equipment, petroleum products, motor vehicles, and clothing. Like many developing nations, Rwanda's exports do not earn the nation enough to offset the cost of these imports. For example, in 2017, the cost of imports amounted to about $1.92 billion, while the revenue from exports totaled $1.05 billion that year. This trade imbalance can force the government deeper into debt every year.

The years of ethnic strife have added to Rwanda's financial plight. For the first two decades of independence—from 1962 to 1980—the country's GDP had grown at a healthy rate of 6.5 percent each year, then dropped to under 3 percent from 1980 to 1985. As the ethnic conflict began, the economy became stagnant, and then its growth rate dropped every year from the late 1980s through 1994. In 1994, the year of the genocide, the GDP declined by a staggering 40 percent. The country and the people were becoming desperately poor.

The decline in Rwanda's finances is reflected in the currency—the Rwandan franc (RWF). In 1999, 334 Rwandan francs equaled 1 U.S. dollar; by 2004, 575 were needed to equal 1 U.S. dollar. In 2020, the exchange rate was about 989 RWF to the dollar.

The fact that Rwanda has been able to reverse the decline in GDP reflects the energy and ability of its people. Peace was established in late 1994, and the GDP grew by 9.5 percent the following year. The growth rate has averaged between 6 and 8 percent since 2003.

Figures on international trade and finance are indicators of how much Rwanda must do to achieve a measure of prosperity. The international community has already offered some help through the International Monetary Fund and the World Bank. Working with these organizations makes it possible for Rwanda's government to spend more money on improvements. In 2019, foreign aid made up 40 percent of Rwanda's national budget.

In addition to international aid, Rwanda has also benefited from massive foreign investments. China has become a crucial partner in Rwanda's bid for economic growth. The country has contributed funding for industrial and government buildings, housing, hospitals, schools, hotels, and important infrastructure through roads, ports, and bridges. Some projects have been gifts from the Chinese government, while others are made possible by loans and investments. While this relationship has fostered unprecedented improvements, many in the international community worry that Rwanda's debt to China may be too great. Recently, Rwanda's debt in relation to its GDP has been rising alarmingly. Many fear that the required interest payments on Chinese debts will take away from funding basic services for Rwandans.

THE FUTURE

One obvious path to economic expansion is achieving growth in foreign tourism, tea exports, and coffee exports. Communications and technology also offer the promise of economic advancement as President Kagame leads the country toward a more service-driven economy. If Rwanda can maintain peace and

Workers at a tea plantation in Kinihira help prepare the product for export.

stability, there's a good chance for growth in all sectors. Kagame is also pushing for new, more sustainable investments from the private rather than the public sector. The production and marketing of tea has been privatized (turned over from a government agency to private companies) under the supervision of a tea board.

While the increase in revenue from tea and coffee production will depend on the world market, the government, often supported by international agencies, is trying to improve the efficiency of other agricultural areas. Some of these efforts, like growing flowers and vegetables for sale in foreign cities, have been slowed by the nation's poor transportation system. Grants from several international agencies and Chinese investments have made it possible to improve existing roads and build new ones. Some new agricultural products that do not require fast shipment, including macadamia nuts, plums, and passion fruit, have increased earnings for many families.

Foreign economists agree that Rwanda's best hope for significant economic growth lies in improving tourism. Some international agencies and even more private companies have invested in services for tourists, including resort hotels and improved facilities and trails in all the parks and national forests. Volcanoes National Park and Akagera National Park have taken center stage in the effort to draw tourists to Rwanda. At Volcanoes National Park, licensed agencies offer guided gorilla treks, following strict regulations to avoid harming these huge, gentle creatures in any way. Veterans of these treks agree that it is one of the most memorable wildlife experiences in Africa, which suggests its potential for contributing to Rwanda's economy.

STUMBLING BLOCKS

Early in 2020, the unexpected catastrophe of COVID-19 began to affect Rwanda. As the virus spread and threatened public health around the world, the resulting closures, travel bans, and impeded flow of goods and services internationally had a damaging impact on Rwanda's economy. The trend for economic growth in Rwanda, which exceeded 9 percent in 2019, has since faltered. It was expected that the total growth for 2020 would be only 2 percent. From July to September 2020 alone, the GDP dropped by 12.4 percent. Travel to Rwanda in 2020 fell by 70 percent, jeopardizing the services sector of the economy. Agriculture was also affected by a drop in demand for exports and lower international prices for crops.

Aid for the public health crisis arrived swiftly from the World Bank, which funded the Rwanda COVID-19 Emergency Response Project with a $14.25 million credit. However, the full extent of the pandemic's impact cannot be measured yet. Since Rwanda's economy relies so prominently on tourism and imported goods, the repercussions of trade and travel restrictions will be deeply felt.

INTERNET LINKS

www.minecofin.gov.rw
The Ministry of Finance and Economic Planning, formed in 1997, works to promote sustainable growth and economic opportunities, and raise the living standards of all Rwandans.

sustainabledevelopment.un.org/content/documents/23432Rwanda_ VNR_Document__Final.pdf
Read about Rwanda's plans for sustainable development beyond 2020.

www.worldbank.org/en/news/feature/2015/03/05/in-rwanda-a-brighter-future-for-miriam
This feature from the World Bank highlights the way new access to electricity has helped small-business owners in Rwanda thrive.

ENVIRONMENT

The struggle for survival has traditionally pitted Rwandans against their environment. In the area around Akagera National Park, cattle-raisers have been vigilant to protect their livestock from lion attacks.

THE REPUBLIC OF RWANDA HAS recognized that it cannot move forward as a stable and prosperous country without a commitment to the environment. The nation's sustainable development goals focus on mitigating climate change and building a safe, clean country free from pollution and destructive land use. Rwanda's vulnerability to climate change has spurred a fierce dedication to clean energy and climate resilience. The country can only achieve a decent standard of living if it has a solid environmental protection program in place.

Ensuring a green future is no small task in Rwanda. The country faces many obstacles to creating a healthier environment. High population density, pollution, land degradation, and fossil fuel dependency pose substantial challenges. The country's history of poverty and conflict also complicates the future.

Poverty and hunger are two great enemies of the environment. People whose daily lives are filled with hunger will destroy portions of their surrounding environment rather than starve. They will allow their livestock to overgraze the land, sacrificing next year's grass so that the

As the extent of environmental degradation has become evident, Rwandans have looked for new ways of supporting their families. Subsistence methods, relied on for generations, were leading to massive deforestation and large ripple effects in the environment. Instead of clearing forests for farming, pastures, and timber, some Rwandans looked to another traditional practice as an alternative method of providing for their families: beekeeping.

In 2016, eight beekeeping cooperatives were created in the Nyabihu district of Rwanda in the area around the Gishwati Mukura National Park. The cooperatives were able to offer training, equipment, and assistance to their members so they could turn this traditional side job into an income generator. Their beekeeping methods provided a sustainable way of living off the land without damaging its forests. The Nyabihu Beekeepers Union grew to 356 members in 2019, all involved in an environmentally friendly trade. Beekeepers actively preserve the environment while also supporting themselves and reducing poverty.

animals can stay alive this year. They will cut down the last tree in order to have fuel to cook their food or heat their homes. The path forward lies in providing education and alternative resources that can help people meet their needs while living more gently on the land.

PRESERVING FORESTS

Every year, more than 2,000 school children visit Akagera National Park for free to learn about environmental conservation.

The loss of forests is one of Rwanda's most urgent environmental problems, and it is connected to other serious problems. Entire forests have been leveled, especially at the end of the 20th century. Large areas of forest were destroyed to create more land for growing crops or for grazing animals. Forests have also been leveled for timber and firewood.

Population pressure has caused a steady reduction in size in all of the country's forested areas. The Nyungwe Forest in the southwest of Rwanda has probably suffered the least, partly because the Belgian government made it a protected reserve in 1933.

Nyungwe is the largest tract of forest left in Rwanda. The Gishwati Forest was about the same size as Nyungwe in the 1930s. However, it was reduced to 1,500 acres (607 hectares) of the original 250,000 (101,171 ha) by 2001. The area was affected by refugees returning to Rwanda who cleared the forests for cropland and pasture. Illegal mining also degraded the land until the creation of Gishwati Mukura National Park in 2015. This park joined the two separate Gishwati and Mukura forests in an effort to restore the landscape and regenerate the forests.

The Akagera region's six lakes and wetlands are home to one of the largest hippopotamus populations in Africa.

Nowhere has the pressure of a dense population been more dramatic than in the Akagera National Park region on Rwanda's eastern border with Tanzania. The park presents the kind of savanna ecosystem seen in movies, with lions, leopards, and other predators following large herds of antelope, buffalo, zebra, and elephant. However, the need for farmland and pastures led to a drastic shrinking of the park, especially after the genocide. Then, many of the returning refugees were given land in and around the park. In 1998 alone, the total park area was reduced by almost two-thirds, from 617,300 acres to 222,200 acres (250,000 ha to 90,000 ha). Much of the remaining parkland was used for fishing camps and cattle grazing.

Akagera's story changed in 2010, when African Parks took over management of the vulnerable refuge. Since then, the nonprofit organization has worked with the government and local community to reclaim and conserve the area, protect surviving wildlife, and reintroduce populations of locally extinct animals. Today, the park has expanded to 277,120 acres (112,146 ha). Educational programs persuade nearby communities that preserving Akagera's forests and wetlands is in their own interest. The parks have also enlisted the help of local communities through a growing number of positions as park rangers and employees.

SEVERE EFFECTS

Damage to one part of an ecosystem has ripple effects through all parts of the system. Deforestation, especially in a mountainous country like Rwanda, leads to soil erosion. Rain washes away precious soil, making it less productive for growing crops and polluting water sources downstream and downhill. Other serious effects are floods and landslides. The danger of landslides is especially great in hilly areas. Planting crops on hillsides without proper terrace farming can be ecologically disastrous. Government agricultural agents try to reduce this danger by showing farm families the value of terraced farming to slow water and soil runoff.

Deforestation also has long-term effects, including climate change. The loss of forests leads to a reduction in rainfall, with less moisture collecting in lakes, ponds, and wetlands. Over time, this produces a warmer, drier climate.

Another long-term effect of deforestation is the loss of biodiversity. One of Rwanda's great treasures is the amazing variety of plant and animal life

Elephants in Akagera National Park have been threatened by poachers interested in their ivory tusks. New protections keep the animals safe within their natural habitat.

it contains. When a forest ecosystem is reduced or destroyed, some species will die out, while animals may migrate to other forested areas.

The loss of forest, savanna, and wetlands in Akagera National Park led many groups of large mammals to move east into Tanzania. Akagera's elephant population declined dramatically in the early 2000s. As conservation planning has transformed the area, the population has risen to about 100. Elephants, mountain gorillas, chimpanzees, and other animals are among the greatest attractions for visitors to Rwanda. Clearly, the country's hopes of attracting tourists is directly tied to the success of environmental conservation and biodiversity protection.

RECOVERING WETLANDS

The pressure of rapid population growth has also led to the dramatic loss of wetlands. Wetlands cover about 10.6 percent of the country's land surface. Currently, the majority of Rwanda's wetlands are used for agriculture. Farm families employ the swampy areas to grow rice and the drier regions to grow vegetables and sugarcane.

The growth of urban areas has added to wetland damage. Building construction, for example, requires wetland resources like sand. Papyrus grown in marshes supplies materials for construction. Some industries have built factories on wetlands to make use of those resources, while other businesses have been dumping toxic waste into the wetlands. Even handicraft industries, such as mat and basket weaving, place an additional burden on wetland resources for raw materials.

Perhaps the greatest danger to the wetlands is the draining of large areas to create land for new settlements and for crops. Draining wetlands means that less water is flowing into streams. In some areas, springs have dried up, and groundwater is very low. Draining can be prevented through strategic farm planning and irrigation. As in the case of deforestation, the shrinking of wetlands contributes to a loss of biodiversity. The protection of both wetlands and forests has become a major 21st-century priority for Rwanda's government and private organizations.

Conservationists are working to safeguard Rugezi Marsh from the effects of deforestation and human activity. The 17,297-acre (7,000 ha) marsh is located in the highlands of northern Rwanda. It is a habitat for a wide variety of plants and animals, especially birds like the ibis and endangered grey crested crane.

Regional deforestation to collect firewood has caused soil erosion and affected the water cycle of Rugezi. Nearby residents have also harvested grasses from the marsh to feed their livestock. These factors endanger Rugezi's habitat and affect water flow through the area. Decreased water flow will have a damaging impact on the two lakes and hydropower plant fed by the Rugezi Marsh.

With protected status as a natural reserve, it is hoped that Rugezi's ecosystem can be rebalanced. Educational programs, reforestation on the surrounding slopes, and innovative agricultural strategies will continue in a movement to rehabilitate the marsh.

Wetlands are a crucial source of water for local communities. They also affect the flow of water into other parts of Rwanda and its border countries.

PROACTIVE PROGRAMS

The Rwandan government has implemented an ambitious program of environmental protection, combining strict laws to reduce damage with projects that will enable Rwandans to gain immediate benefits from conservation. The government has received a good deal of financial and technical help from environmental agencies in Rwanda and from international organizations, including the UN and the World Bank.

Reforestation programs have replanted thousands of acres of trees along roads, on private farms, in national parks, and on public land. To protect the trees from disease, a variety of species are planted, including eucalyptus, lemon, and acacia. Rwanda plans to reforest 4.9 million acres (2 million ha) of land by 2030. The country is also developing agroforestry, or agricultural methods that incorporate tree conservation and cultivation. Reforestation programs work especially well when combined with programs to provide alternatives to wood for cooking fuel, such as solar-powered ovens.

New laws have been passed to reduce the degradation of both forests and wetlands. For example, Rwanda Environmental Management Authority (REMA) has control over all use of wetlands; any new wetland activity requires written approval from REMA.

Wherever possible, the government tries to combine environmental protection programs with profit-making programs. In urban areas, for example, Rwanda faced a serious problem with the disposal of solid wastes, especially in Kigali. This posed a great threat to delicate wetland ecosystems. With technical assistance from the former Kigali Institute of Science, Technology and Management (KIST), several women's associations established special dump sites where they process garbage into fertilizers and household cooking fuels. Garbage became a money-making venture for the women, and Kigali has gained a reputation as a remarkably clean capital city.

In 2008, the country took a giant step when it banned non-biodegradable plastic bags. The law is so strict that travelers arriving in Rwanda have their possessions searched for the item and can face large fines. By controlling plastic bags, the government is able to prevent people from burning bags, disposing of them inappropriately, and contributing to pollution. Now, Rwanda is working toward becoming a plastic-free country.

CLIMATE CHANGE

Rwanda has committed on national, regional, and global levels to sustainable development and environmental actions that will combat climate change. It joined more than 80 other nations in ratifying the Paris Agreement on Climate Change in 2015. Since then, Rwanda has continued to assess its progress and pledge new action to reduce greenhouse gas emissions.

Rwanda is uniquely susceptible to the effects of climate change. Wide variations in temperature and rainfall are risky for a nation that depends so heavily on agricultural success and already has a history of land degradation. Floods, landslides, and droughts have become more frequent because of climate change. Millions have died in Rwanda over the past few decades as a result. These severe natural disasters have also devastated crops, farmland, and important infrastructure.

A power plant captures methane from Lake Kivu to use in the production of nitrogen fertilizer and fuel for trucks. Methane is naturally produced by decaying matter in the lake.

Rwanda contributes only a small fraction of the greenhouse gas emissions that are altering the climate so dramatically. However, the country has made it a priority to reduce emissions by 5 million tons (4.6 million tonnes) by 2030. The plan involves a more efficient transportation sector, new agricultural practices, a shift away from traditional fuels, and investments in renewable energy. Instead of burning firewood and biomass, Rwanda is hoping to make the switch to solar and hydropower solutions.

Solar energy is a promising source of electricity for rural Rwandans. Just over half the population has access to electricity, but solar systems can revolutionize education, business enterprises, and homelife. The government is working with solar energy companies to set up off-grid systems that can reach remote villages and communities.

Rwanda's government understands that its economic future is closely linked with environmental health. A higher standard of living for Rwandans cannot be attained without sustainable environmental policies. Connecting the entire country to renewable energy sources, adopting green practices, and protecting natural ecosystems can help the nation achieve its environmental and socioeconomic goals.

INTERNET LINKS

www.dw.com/en/ambitious-goals-for-reforestation-in-rwanda/av-46125430
A video from DW, a broadcasting company in Germany, chronicles Rwanda's strategic reforestation goals and techniques.

pulitzercenter.org/reporting/rwanda-elephant-chief
Read the story of Mutware—an elephant with a big personality that lived in Akagera National Park from 1975 until his death in 2018.

www.rema.gov.rw
Check the Rwanda Environment Management Authority's website for news about new conservation projects and policies.

RWANDANS

The people of Rwanda have worked hard at reconciliation in order to embrace a brighter future for the next generation of Rwandans.

INHABITANTS OF RWANDA ARE CALLED Banyarwanda. They speak the same language, have the same culture, live on the same hills, and, for centuries, have intermarried. The three ethnic groups are the Bahutu, the Batutsi, and the Batwa, referred to in the West as Hutus, Tutsis, and Twas. However, Rwanda has banned the use of these ethnic labels.

When Rwanda exploded into civil war and then the genocide of 1994, people in the United States and other countries were puzzled by the early TV-news accounts of "death squads" roaming the countryside, brutally murdering men, women, and children. Who was doing the killing, and who were the victims? Why were Rwandans killing each other?

Many Rwandans were also bewildered. They could not understand the wholesale slaughter that made victims of even the youngest children. In spite of tensions between the Hutu and the Tutsi, there was a widespread belief that ethnic differences could be overcome. After all, there was a good deal of intermarriage between the two groups, so how could one group try to destroy the other? The victims themselves often had no idea why they were being attacked. One often-repeated account of the genocide tells of a group of schoolgirls who were told by a death squad to divide into Hutu and Tutsi, with the understanding that Hutu would be spared. The girls refused to divide, insisting instead that they were all Rwandans. They were all murdered.

6

"Every citizen has a tough story. When we see Rwandans laughing, talking to each other, it is a miracle."

—Samuel Munyaneza, guide at Akagera National Park

What led to such blind rage? How could members of the death squads convince themselves that they were justified in butchering every Tutsi in sight and any Hutu who seemed sympathetic toward them? The seeds of hatred were deeply rooted in Rwanda's past.

ETHNIC GROUPS

Rwanda no longer recognizes ethnic groups, but it is estimated that about 84 percent of the population are Hutu and 15 percent are Tutsi. A third group, the Twa or Batwa, were the first indigenous group in Rwanda and make up less than 1 percent of the population. Both the Hutu and the Tutsi are Bantu-speaking groups who share a common culture and language.

Of the two main groups, the Hutu arrived in the region first, beginning around the 5th century. Throughout history, most Hutu were farmers, growing crops and raising some livestock—goats, sheep, and cattle.

Because Rwanda has no written history, it is impossible to say when the Tutsi first arrived or where they came from. From the oral tradition of the people, historians believe the Tutsi made their appearance around the 14th century. Unlike the agricultural Hutu, the Tutsi were nomadic pastoralists, or herders, who relied on their cattle for food.

The Tutsi quickly gained power over the Hutu and dominated the feudal system called ubuhake. In the ubuhake system, wealth and the power of being an overlord or master were based on the number of cattle owned. The Tutsi herders, being cattle owners, were often in positions of power, although the Hutu, and even some Twa, could acquire cattle by purchase, by war, or by marriage. With this system firmly in place, the Tutsi formed a dominant class similar to the nobility of Europe, and the Hutu were a large underclass of peasant farmers. People could switch positions—Hutu could join the Tutsi class and vice versa.

All Tutsi kings were descended from one ruling clan.

By the 20th century, there were other modifications to the ubuhake system. A number of Tutsi worked in business or in government posts. The king, or mwami, was invariably Tutsi. Also, some Hutus left farming to work in towns, and some became potters.

Although this feudal system placed the Hutu in a position of almost permanent inferiority, there was little evidence of rebellion. Intermarriage was common. Any Hutu resentment seems to have been minimal until the 20th century, when the period of German and Belgian rule brought points of friction into the open.

This man lives in what has traditionally been a Hutu village. Classifications of Hutu and Tutsi have been banned in order to avoid problematic distinctions between "perpetrators" and "victims."

COLONIAL CATEGORIES

Rwanda was part of Germany's colonial empire for less than 20 years, but this was long enough to expose the tension between the Hutu and Tutsi. In 1911 and 1912, the Germans joined with the Tutsi monarchy to conquer two Hutu areas in the north. The Hutu were proud of their independence and fought vigorously before being forced to surrender. Their resentment seethed until after independence was achieved in 1962.

Belgium took control of the two areas that became Rwanda and Burundi in 1916, and in 1919, Belgium was entrusted with the area as a League of Nations mandate. After World War II and the creation of the UN, Ruanda-Urundi became a UN Trust Territory under Belgium's leadership. Belgium had become a major colonial power in Africa in the 19th century and controlled the much larger Belgian Congo to the west. The Belgians had a strict program for "civilizing" colonial peoples, and they applied these ideas to Rwandans between 1916 and 1962, when Rwanda became an independent nation.

During the nearly half century of Belgian rule, the Europeans had considerable success in improving physical aspects of the area. For example, teams of agricultural specialists fanned out across Rwanda and showed farm families how to increase production by using improved seeds and chemical

This Tutsi woman lost her entire family during the genocide. The Tutsi people underwent a dramatic reversal in Rwandan history, from members of a small, aristocratic class to victims of a brutal genocide.

fertilizers. Most importantly, they taught the Hutu men and women how to shape hillsides into terraces to avoid disastrous soil erosion. In terms of human relations, however, the Belgians fueled the simmering tensions between the Hutu and the Tutsi. They undermined the authority of the mwami by using Belgian officials instead of his trusted Tutsi administrators. Then, following a 1948 UN report critical of the low status of the Hutu and the Twa, more attention was paid to providing opportunities for the Hutu.

In the 1950s, the Hutu themselves began demanding a stronger voice in government, and in 1954, the ubuhake system was officially abolished. At the same time, the Catholic Church became a major supporter of the Hutu and encouraged them to become involved in the political process. Quite suddenly, the Belgians, who had always supported the powerful Tutsi minority, switched their loyalty to the Hutu.

Once independence was achieved and the Hutu majority controlled the government, Rwanda's two main ethnic groups experienced a great role reversal. After dominating society, the economy, and the government for several hundred years, the Tutsi became a virtually powerless minority. The Hutu, formerly regarded as a lower class, were now determined to solidify their dominance. The Tutsi were to be limited to 9 percent of positions in schools, businesses, and government, reflecting the fact that they accounted for that percentage of the population. To make this quota system work, the Hutu relied on one of the legacies of Belgian rule: identity cards that stated whether the cardholder was Hutu, Tutsi, or of mixed ethnicity.

In the early 1900s, some Europeans engaged in a pseudoscience called eugenics to categorize racial and ethnic groups according to physical

EUGENICS IN RWANDA

In the early 1930s, the Belgians launched a census to categorize all Rwandans. Many people, especially the Hutu, felt humiliated by "scientists," armed with calipers, measuring tapes, scales, and charts, spending hours measuring them from head to toe. When a clear categorization could not be made because intermarriage had led to ethnic blending, the census taker made a judgment. If the person seemed well educated or prosperous, he or she was labeled Tutsi.

In 1935, the Belgian government issued identity cards for all Rwandans. These identity cards became standard from that time on. During the genocide in 1994, identification cards were sometimes checked at roadblocks to identify Tutsi citizens. They were one more indicator of who would be killed and who would be spared.

characteristics, such as height, bone structure, and coloring, in order to "improve" and rank the quality of races. It was this pseudoscience that led the leaders of Nazi Germany to describe Aryan Germans as a "superior race," while other groups, such as Jews, Slavs, and Roma (once known by the now-derogatory term "Gypsies"), were deemed inferior. In Rwanda, first the Germans and then the Belgians were struck by physical differences between the Hutu and Tutsi. The Europeans believed that the Tutsi tended to be quite tall and slender. The Hutu, on the other hand, were usually shorter and squatter. The Twa were even shorter in stature.

Some ethnic classifications were made based on livestock ownership; if a person had more than 10 cows, they were considered Tutsi.

BATWA

The Batwa, once called Pygmies (a term now considered to be derogatory), are the descendants of the original residents of what is now Rwanda. Their numbers today are estimated at about 33,000—less than 1 percent of the total population. The Batwa, or Twa, as they are more commonly known, lived for centuries as hunters and gatherers. Their traditional culture is rich in dance and music, and they are closely related to forest people in other countries of central Africa. When the Hutu moved in and established farms, the Twa moved primarily to mountain slopes and forests.

During the period of the Rwandan kingdoms, some emerged from the forests to become potters. The Twa were present in the royal court, often as entertainers and dancers. They became famous for a dance they performed with Tutsi dancers.

In the 1980s and 1990s, the Twa were forced from their homes to make way for forest conservation. Lands in Volcanoes National Park, Nyungwe Forest Reserve, and Gishwati Forest were taken over by the government, leaving the Twa with no choice but to move and lose much of the traditional forest knowledge they had depended on for centuries. The lack of land deepened the extent of poverty in Twa communities.

Very few Twa people own farmland or cattle. Most live in extreme poverty and try to find informal work as potters or day laborers.

The Twa suffered severely during the genocide. Many Hutus viewed the Twa as sympathetic to the Tutsi, and they were targeted for violence. An estimated 30 percent were killed, compared with 14 percent of the population overall. A similar number fled Rwanda. Many Twa feel that their story is left out of the official commemorations of genocide victims.

The Twa have faced a great deal of prejudice. They have usually been stigmatized as inferior and have lived in extreme poverty. They have unequal access to housing, education, health care, and employment, and Twa women are especially affected. Many believe that the government's failure to recognize ethnicity has had a devastating impact on Twa communities. International critics believe the Twa should be able to self-identify as an indigenous ethnic group. However, the Rwandan government has denied funding for any groups claiming indigenous or Twa identity. Without recognition of their marginalized status, it will be difficult for the Twa people to access the resources and representation they need.

BANYARWANDA

Since 1995, the Rwandan people have been committed to overcoming the stereotypes concerning ethnic differences that led to conflict and violence. Reeducation camps for returning refugees and perpetrators drove home the idea that all Rwandans are one. In order to promote reconciliation and a future-oriented perspective, the government has emphasized the sameness of the people without mentioning the differences. All Rwandans are now Banyarwanda and nothing more, at least in the public sphere. This has mixed results and has been met with both praise and criticism.

The government's policies have raised many questions about whether it is wise or even possible to eliminate ethnicity entirely from a society. Prejudices persist despite the official line that "We are all Rwandans now." The ban on ethnicity covers up potentially harmful social divisions and puts off a difficult discussion instead of facing it head on. Some say that it represses identity and severely limits freedom of expression in Rwanda.

News reports of discrimination or prejudice are common, and international organizations record some abuses, especially of the Twa. Those who speak of ethnicity can be fined or jailed for the crime of "divisionism." Many fear that this is just another way of limiting and punishing political opposition and unwanted media.

INTERNET LINKS

www.britannica.com/topic/Hutu
Encyclopedia Britannica offers an overview of the Hutu people.

www.britannica.com/topic/Tutsi
The article describes the history and culture of the Tutsi people of Rwanda and Burundi.

minorityrights.org/minorities/twa-2/
This page from Minority Rights describes the discrimination and challenges facing the Twa people today in Rwanda.

LIFESTYLE

Children under age 15 make up about
40 percent of Rwanda's population.

7

EVERYDAY LIFE IN RWANDA HAS changed dramatically since the genocide. At first, the focus was on rebuilding. Rwanda made rapid progress to regain its footing after the genocide, and now the positive momentum continues. The country has far exceeded the standard of living enjoyed by citizens before the conflict, and it has set even higher goals moving forward.

Rebuilding after the conflict involved restoring houses, businesses, and even entire villages and towns. Much of the capital city, Kigali, was destroyed. Workers in businesses and government offices returned in late 1994 to find office machines wrecked and tons of files destroyed or strewn in all directions.

More importantly, the rebuilding involved restoring a way of life. The traumatic loss of life in the 1994 genocide was accompanied by the loss of jobs, land, and communities. The survivors could not simply return to the way things had been. Too many loved ones had been lost, and families had been torn apart. Many widows, aided and encouraged by international agencies, created households consisting of three or more women and up to a dozen orphans. Older children often became "parents" to younger siblings.

In spite of the upheaval, most Rwandans seemed to go about the task of reconstructing their lives with surprising energy and hope. Government

New building projects have brought modern apartment complexes to Kigali, although they are only available to more wealthy Rwandans.

Rwandan lawmakers have proposed limiting the number of children a family can have in order to stem population growth.

agencies and international organizations have provided various kinds of assistance. More than 25 years after the conflict, Rwandans have restored stability and spurred progress.

EVERYDAY LIFE

More than 80 percent of the Rwandan people live in rural areas. The typical rural community is usually not a defined village, such as those found in rural America. Instead, most people live in a *rugo*, a traditional homestead consisting of several beehive-shaped houses within a larger family compound. These family compounds, in turn, are scattered over the seemingly endless hills that make up the landscape of Rwanda.

The most important family house, usually the home of a respected elder, is in the middle of the compound. The traditional houses are made of woven branches and grasses and are covered with smooth clay. Windows and doors are set in wooden frames. In the 21st century, modern Western-style houses have become more common, although the layout of the compounds remains the same. Each house is surrounded by a fence, usually made of thick bushes.

In Kinyarwanda, the language of Rwanda, the word *inzu* can refer to a family, a household, or a house. The term usually means a husband and wife, their children, and other close relatives. Large families are common, and a family without children is thought to be incomplete, an object of pity. When people from several inzu can trace their origins to a common male ancestor, they form a kinship unit called an *umuryango*, which is led by the oldest and most respected male.

KIGALI

Kigali was a small farm town until Rwanda gained independence in 1962. As the country prepared for independence, most people thought Butare, now called Huye, would be named the capital. After all, it had been the administrative center of Rwanda during Belgian rule. Kigali was chosen instead, probably because of its central location, and that choice led to explosive growth. From a town of a few thousand, Kigali now has a population of 1.2 million.

The city was originally built on a ridge and now extends down both hillsides to the valley floors and onto a second ridge. Kigali today is remarkably neat and clean, the streets lined with flowering trees and shrubs. Although heavily damaged in 1994, much of it has been rebuilt, and a construction boom has been underway since the late 1990s.

Kimironko market in Kigali is a popular attraction for locals and international visitors. Vendors sell food, clothing, and handicrafts.

The business and social center of the city is colorful, noisy, and bustling with activity. The pace slows down for an hour or two in the early afternoon. Foreign and Rwandan businesspeople dressed in business attire share the crowded streets with Rwandans dressed in traditional clothing or in casual Western-style clothes. Upscale restaurants cater to Rwandan businesspeople and the many representatives of international agencies in the city.

A newer section of the city, located on another hill, houses government and administrative offices. Many of the buildings display striking 21st-century architecture, much of it designed by Rwandan architects. Kigali City Tower is a prominent 20-story skyscraper completed in 2011 that dominates the cityscape. Gifts and investments from the Chinese government have also led to new building projects, like the prime minister's office unveiled in 2019.

Outside of the business and tourist center, tree-lined residential streets extend down the hills. Many of the houses look more like modern houses in Europe or America.

CITY LIVING

Kigali is by far the largest city in Rwanda. Another important city is Butare, or Huye as it is officially named. The city is often called the intellectual center of Rwanda, largely because it was the site of the National University of Rwanda.

COMMUNITY SERVICE

Residents of Kigali practice a form of community service that brings local communities together and keeps the neighborhoods of the capital city clean. This practice is called umuganda, *which means "coming together." On the last Saturday of every month, at least one member of each household spends the morning cleaning up their neighborhood. Anyone between the ages of 18 and 65 is eligible to help. The practice began in 1998, and it was signed into law about a decade later. Today, the neighborhoods, or cells as they are called, use WhatsApp to coordinate their efforts. Kigali is often celebrated for its clean streets, and* umuganda *is the civic and social practice that makes its high standards possible.*

The majority of roads in Rwanda are unpaved, even in the busy capital city of Kigali.

This was the nation's first university, founded in 1963. After the reorganization of provinces in 2006, Butare's name was changed to Huye. However, many Rwandans still refer to its original name.

The pace of life is slower in Huye than in Kigali. However, the marketplace, where vendors sell all sorts of clothing, hardware, and foods, is busy, crowded, and noisy. It is full of the sound of drums from the performances or practices of traditional dance troupes.

Huye is also the home of the Ethnographic Museum of Rwanda, which houses displays on Rwandan history and culture. The museum, which opened in 1989, was a gift from the king of Belgium to celebrate the country's independence. It is regarded as one of the best museums in East Africa for its presentation of archaeological and historical information.

Other towns in Rwanda serve mostly as administrative centers. Some house foreign visitors working with various aid organizations. A number of towns, such as Gikongoro and Rubavu, are gaining new businesses designed to attract and serve tourists. A few others, such as Karongi and Rusizi, on Lake Kivu, serve as fishing ports and beach towns. The cities of Muhanga, Nyagatare, and Musanze are rising urban centers in Rwanda.

RURAL COMMUNITIES

Most Rwandan families live by farming. For many, daily life is a struggle to get enough food from the basic crops grown and the small livestock (primarily goats and sheep) raised. Cattle are raised as both symbols of wealth and status and for food. Most Rwandans eat meat only two or three times a month. Their basic diet consists of vegetables, fruit, and grain (such as millet or corn).

Many rural people combine making handicrafts with raising crops to make a living. The Twas, for example, are famous for their pottery. Others, both Hutu and Tutsi, are wood carvers, while still others make furniture, fabrics, or musical instruments.

Traditional homes in Rwanda were round huts made from natural materials like grasses, bamboo, and reeds. Now, many houses in Rwanda follow a more Western style.

Clothing styles are changing as low-cost European and American designs become more readily available. Many people continue to prefer traditional clothing, men in loose-fitting white garments and women in brightly colored wraps. Geometric designs commonly decorate Rwandan textiles.

Fridays are market days in Rwandan villages and cities. Stalls offer a striking array of merchandise, including cattle, sheep, goats, and pigs, as well as vegetables, fruits, clothing, and housewares. There are stacks of mattresses with bright, floral-print covers; recycled pots and pans; and handmade, unpainted furniture. Loud music blares both African and international sounds. The activity is colorful and lively, and the market offers people the chance to see old friends and make new ones.

FAMILIES

The family is central to Rwandan life, so it is traditionally expected that every woman will marry. Polygamy used to be common in Rwanda, but it is now illegal. The median age of first marriage for women is 23, and it is typical for

Huye, or Butare, has been known by many names. Between 1935 and 1962, it was called Astrida after Belgium's Princess Astrid.

TRADITIONAL AND HISTORIC CLOTHING

Hides from goats and cows were used to make clothing in Rwanda's earliest days. Animal skins were dried in the sun, softened with water, stretched, and then cut and stitched into garments. Some items were also made from pounded bark.

Most clothing items served a primarily practical purpose. The isinde, *for example, is a sort of jacket constructed from woven wicker or straw. It provided protection from the rain for cow herders. Other special headdresses and outfits were reserved for ceremonial dances and occasions.*

Although Western-style clothing has become more common, you can still see traditional garments worn for dances and events. The mushanana *is a traditional dress for Rwandan women that is remerging as a popular style. The look is achieved with a large piece of fabric that is tied around the waist and then draped over one shoulder.*

Most weddings in Rwanda are broken up into multiple parts: a traditional ceremony, a religious ceremony, and the civil ceremony that makes the union legally binding.

families to place pressure on a woman if she has not married by her late 20s. The median age of first marriage for men is 26.

When a couple wishes to marry in the traditional manner, the groom's family first pays a bride-price to the bride's father, usually giving a cow or other livestock. A couple can dissolve a marriage if both agree and if the bride-price is returned to the groom's family. Over the past few decades, couples have been marrying later, sometimes in their 30s. The delay is usually because the couple does not have land for starting a farm or else the groom cannot afford the bride-price.

Other family traditions have also given way to the pressures of modern life. In the past, for example, after a child was born, both the mother and infant remained in seclusion for eight days. On the day they reentered family life, relatives gave presents to the new parents, and the baby was introduced to the family. When the infant was three or four months old, a naming ceremony was held. Only the most traditional families continue these practices.

EDUCATIONAL GOALS

Education in the primary grades is free, and officially at least, it is compulsory for children ages 7 through 12. In reality, enrollment never reaches 100 percent. It has repeatedly come close since 2001.

Secondary and technical school enrollment has not kept pace, however, with only about 14 percent of eligible students enrolled. The low secondary school enrollment is reflected in another statistic: Only 73.2 percent of adults are literate (able to read and write).

Language has added a complicating factor. The spoken language of Rwanda is Kinyarwanda, a Bantu language, but the official written languages are French and English. Instruction used to be provided in both French and English, with education at the university level limited to French. In 2008, the government changed that policy so that English technically became the language of instruction for all levels of education.

Many Rwandans are aware of the vital role education plays in building a modern nation. Education at all levels was hit hard during the 1990s, when most schools and the university closed their doors. It was not until 1995 or later that primary and secondary schools began to reopen. The National University of Rwanda in Huye (formerly Butare) opened in 1963 and had about 2,500 students

The number of students attending secondary school has increased since 2009.

The headquarters of the University of Rwanda is in Kigali. The tall buildings pictured in the distance belong to the university.

in 1990. After being shut down for much of the decade, the university gradually returned to normal. Thousands of teachers and students were killed in the genocide, and Rwanda had difficulty finding enough qualified teachers. Volunteers from other countries helped fill the gaps.

In 2013, the National University merged with other higher-education institutions. The resulting University of Rwanda is composed of six separate, specialized colleges. Different schools are dedicated to science and technology, agriculture and animal husbandry, finance and banking, health and medicine, and arts and sciences. They operate through 14 campuses around the country.

The government has established several programs to encourage women to go to school and to enter the world of business. Some of the goals set for the early 21st century are to establish more literacy programs outside the schools, to end discrimination against school-age mothers, to improve education in preventing sexually transmitted diseases such as HIV/AIDS, and to provide more help for women living in poverty. Rwanda has welcomed help from international organizations as it works to meet these goals.

HEALTH CARE

Radical economic change has transformed daily life for many Rwandans. In 2019, though, 43 percent of the population still lived below the international poverty line, with 16 percent living in extreme poverty. Like other low-income countries, Rwanda has struggled to provide adequate health care for its citizens. However, Rwandans now have universal health coverage, which means that citizens can get the services they need without financial hardship.

The Rwandan government has partnered with international donors and taken a vigorous approach to making health care more easily accessible to all Rwandans. A special focus is needed for poor, rural communities that lack basic resources and have fewer trained health-care workers. The health-care system employs community health workers as the first point of access for those seeking medical care.

Another focus has been on raising awareness and teaching disease prevention. Malaria, tuberculosis, and HIV/AIDS have typically had high rates in Rwanda, but they have all declined in recent years. Vaccination rates in Rwanda are another success, exceeding 93 percent. Vaccines offer valuable protections against contagious diseases, especially for children.

There are many signs of improving health in Rwanda. The life expectancy has lengthened in the past 20 years, maternal and infant mortality rates are lower, and rates of communicable diseases have dropped. Nutrition is still a challenge, especially for children. Around 38 percent of children under five are malnourished. Providing nutritious food and clean water to all citizens is an important area for growth in Rwanda's future.

When COVID-19 entered the region in 2020, Rwanda combated the new virus by adapting some of the systems it already had in place for treating HIV/AIDS, malaria, and other diseases. The country responded quickly with clear national leadership, virus tracking, strict lockdowns, and a mask mandate. Robots were used to screen and test people for the virus and deliver supplies in special COVID clinics. Consistent guidelines and strict enforcement of mask rules have helped to keep the case load relatively low, despite the fact that just 5 percent of Rwandan households have a place for handwashing with soap and water. In 2020, Rwanda counted a total of 8,383 cases and 92 deaths from COVID-19.

Rwanda uses advanced technology, like robots and drones, to deliver medical supplies.

INTERNET LINKS

kigalicity.gov.rw
Kigali City's official website provides information about regular events, like Kigali Car Free Day, and attractions.

www.unicef.org/rwanda/water-sanitation-and-hygiene
UNICEF analyzes the availability of clean water and sanitation in Rwanda on this website.

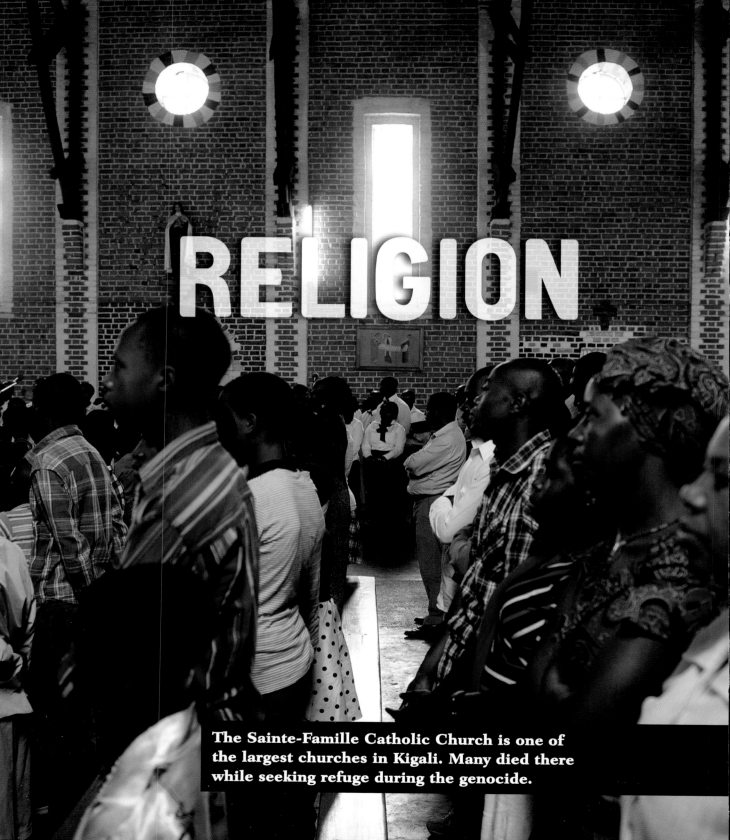

RELIGION

The Sainte-Famille Catholic Church is one of the largest churches in Kigali. Many died there while seeking refuge during the genocide.

RELIGION IN RWANDA HAS THREE main influences: tribal religions, Christianity, and Islam. Tribal religions dominated life in Rwanda until the arrival of Europeans at the end of the 19th century. Then, Christianity became widespread during the colonial period. Since the genocide, some Rwandans have converted to Islam.

Christianity has had a strong impact on Rwandan life since German and Belgian missionaries arrived. By the 1920s, more than half the people had become Roman Catholic. Protestant missionaries have also gained converts and, today, various evangelical churches have been very successful, especially the Seventh-day Adventists.

Traditional, or tribal, religions have never disappeared, and many Rwandans seem to combine tribal traditions with Christian practices and beliefs. This mixing makes it difficult to determine the exact number of followers of each religion or denomination. According to the most recent calculations from the CIA, 49.5 percent of Rwandans are Protestant, followed by 43.7 percent Roman Catholic, and 2 percent Muslim. Less than 1 percent subscribe to other belief systems, and 2.5 percent don't follow any religion. It is believed that a portion of the population continues to adhere to traditional religions, even though they also worship at a Christian church or an Islamic mosque.

CHRISTIAN VISIONS

In 1981, a teenage girl named Alphonsine Mumereke saw visions of the Virgin Mary at the village of Kibeho. The visions continued with two of her friends. The Catholic Church acknowledged these apparitions, and the village drew pilgrims, first from Rwanda, then from other countries.

The village suffered terribly during and after the genocide, and its church was burned while sheltering refugees. Sightings of the Virgin, known as Our Lady of Kibeho, have since resumed. Many visitors have been struck by the fact that such sightings have occurred on the eve of great warfare and destruction. For example, the visions of Mary began at Medjugorje in Yugoslavia just before that country exploded in civil war in the mid-1980s.

A church honoring Our Lady of Kibeho also commemorates the thousands who died in the village during massacres in 1994 and 1995.

TRADITIONAL RELIGION

The traditional religion of Rwanda provides a number of clues that help explain why the people so readily accepted Christianity. Rwandans have always believed in a supreme being, for example, called Imana. This god figure controls the entire world, but Rwanda is his home, and he returns there every night to rest. Many people continue to follow time-honored rituals involving Imana. The very name Imana is thought to have magical powers, so Rwandans often make use of it in naming children, as well as in sayings designed for such things as comfort, blessing, or promise. "Imana has blessed me with a son," would be a typical reference to this spiritual power, as would "May Imana make my cattle survive the disease."

Imana's name and power are also part of folktales and sayings. Many of these stories tell of people who received great gifts from Imana, then lost everything because they were greedy or disloyal.

These traditional beliefs also involve an element of fatalism, or the idea that events are part of a person's destiny. This idea of destiny begins early in a person's life. When a woman wants to become pregnant, for example, she places a few drops of water in a pitcher each night. This is in keeping with the notion that Imana is a potter who needs water to mix with the clay in the woman's womb.

When the child is born, Imana decides whether this person's life will be basically happy or troubled. Of course, people do not know right away what has been decided for this person. In time, though, if the individual is stricken with illness, falls into debt, or has a failed marriage, then people are likely to say that this person was created by Ruremakwaci. This is a name that describes Imana when, for whatever reason, he decides that a certain destiny will not be a happy one.

Another aspect of traditional religion that Rwandans can incorporate into their Christian beliefs is the idea of a life force, or soul, that remains in existence after a person dies. An animal's life force supposedly disappears at death, but in humans it turns into *bazimu*. These spirits of the dead reside in an underworld, Ikuzimu, and they keep the personality and even the name of the living person. Their existence is neither happy nor sad, but they do tend to linger around the places they once inhabited. The bazimu may live in the family home or in special huts made for them.

Most of the time, people are not pleased to feel that these spirits are present. They are said to bring illness, poor harvests, and poverty, most likely because they can no longer enjoy the pleasures of this life. Their power over people is limited to members of their own clan, and troubled family members usually consult a diviner who may be able to send the spirit back to the underworld.

CHRISTIANITY

Roman Catholic churches in Rwanda all seem to be large, like the enormous cathedral of Kabgayi, a few miles from Gitarama. It is the oldest in the country

An unusual cult from traditional Rwandan religion surrounded the mythical figure of Ryangombe. According to legend, Ryangombe was a great warrior killed by a rampaging bull. His distraught friends threw themselves onto the horns of the bull to join him. Imana gave Ryangombe and his followers a special place as bazimu: the Karisimbi volcano in the Virunga chain of volcanoes.

In the past, this cult seemed to be a unifying force in Rwandan society. A sort of brotherhood developed that included Hutu, Tutsi, and Twa members. Rituals and dances were held every July to honor Ryangombe, for which the members of the brotherhood painted their bodies and decorated special spirit huts. One member represented the spirit of Ryangombe and carried his spear. Even though the cult is disappearing in the early 21st century, it is remembered fondly for its idealistic encouragement of national unity and personal honor.

and completed in 1925. Even before the cathedral was built, missionaries were installed in Kabgayi in 1905, and it became the seat of Rwanda's first Catholic bishop.

Services in Kabgayi are well attended. Rwandans, with their love of music and dance, have always responded well to the colorful robes, the Gregorian chants, the processions, and the music. In the decades before independence, there were also training schools, where Rwandans could develop skills in areas such as carpentry, furniture making, printing, and blacksmithing. The Kabgayi Church Museum preserves the cultural history of the region as well as early religious artifacts.

Rwanda's largest cathedral is in Huye. The red-brick structure was built in the 1930s to honor Belgium's Princess Astrid. Visitors are often struck by the peacefulness of the enormous interior when the cathedral is empty. During services, the sounds echo upward, adding to the beauty of the mass.

The role of Christian churches during the civil war and genocide is ambiguous. Many officials encouraged Hutu leaders in their drive for political power after independence, and some facilitated the violence of the genocide.

"We apologize for all the wrongs the church committed (during the genocide). We apologize on behalf of all Christians for all forms of wrongs we committed."
—Conference of Catholic Bishops, 2016

On the other hand, many nuns, priests, and pastors died trying to protect others.

Tutsi and Hutu moderates flocked to the churches for protection in 1994. In too many instances, Hutu death squads trapped victims inside churches, tossed grenades through the windows, then killed survivors with guns and machetes. Church officials were helpless to stop the slaughter, and some sided with the militia.

In 2016, the Catholic Church in Rwanda released a statement publicly apologizing for the Church's role in the genocide. The apology mentioned both acts of violence and the failure to stop the massacres and hatred. Before this statement, the Church had not admitted to any complicity in the mass killings. Many saw the apology as a sign of hope for true reconciliation.

Rwandans worship at Chapel Mbyo. The Chapel is located in a "reconciliation village," one of the places in Rwanda where victims and perpetrators lived side by side after the genocide.

ISLAM

Disappointment and betrayal marred the relationship many Rwandans had with the Catholic Church after the genocide. As they questioned their faith in Christian institutions, many began seriously exploring Islam. Some Rwandans had found shelter and safety in mosques, Muslim houses of worship, during the killings. Muslims had modeled compassion and courage through the crisis and helped to hide and rescue their neighbors.

At the time of the genocide, the Muslim community was small but well established. The religion was probably brought to the country by Arab Muslim merchants in the 19th century, and the first mosque in the country was built

Boys study the Quran, the holy book of Islam, at a special school in Kigali.

in 1913. Following the genocide, Islam became the fastest growing religion in Rwanda. Despite the official count of 2 percent, it is believed that Muslims could make up as much as 10 percent of the population.

Islam was founded in the 7th century by the Arab prophet Muhammad. Islam shares some beliefs with both Christianity and Judaism, including the belief in one god. Muslims also accept such Hebrew prophets as Abraham and Moses, and they regard Jesus Christ as another great prophet, while Muhammad is considered the last and most important prophet.

Muslims are required to practice the Five Pillars of Islam: to recite the profession of faith at least once; to respond to the five daily calls to public prayer; to pay a special tax to support the poor; to fast every day during the holy month of Ramadan; and to perform, if they are able, the *hajj*, or pilgrimage, to the holy city of Mecca in Saudi Arabia.

Genocide memorials have been built throughout Rwanda, but churches are also common places to commemorate the victims. Threatened Rwandans fled to local churches for refuge during the conflict. Instead of being places of safety, too many became sites of massacres. Some churches, like the hilltop church at Kibuye on Lake Kivu, remained damaged and empty for several years. The scarred building served as memorial to the victims. Now, the church is open for religious services, and a genocide memorial has been constructed next to it.

At a memorial in Ntarama, the church was left just as it was after around 5,000 bodies were removed in 1994. The scraps of clothing and personal items on the floor are powerful reminders of the tragic event. Like the display of victims' skulls and bones in other memorials, these disturbing artifacts make certain that no one in the future can claim there was no genocide.

In a bustling neighborhood of shops and stalls in southern Kigali, a muezzin's voice is heard issuing the Muslim call to public prayer. Nearby, a large mosque looms above the busy street. This neighborhood in Kigali, known as Nyamirambo, is the place where the Muslim presence in Rwanda is most visible.

INTERNET LINKS

www.newtimes.co.rw/news/seventh-day-adventist-community-rwanda-celebrate-centenary-jubilee
This article from Rwanda's *New Times* describes the celebrations accompanying the 100th anniversary of Seventh-day Adventists in the country.

www.worldatlas.com/articles/religious-beliefs-in-rwanda.html
World Atlas breaks down the different religious associations within Rwanda and how they interact with each other.

LANGUAGE

Travelers entering Rwanda from Tanzania are welcomed to the country by a sign written in Kinyarwanda, French, and English.

9

LANGUAGE AND COMMUNICATION methods have undergone important changes in Rwanda recently. The languages used in Rwanda have shifted at critical points throughout its history to reflect a changing nation. Now, communication has been revolutionized with mobile phones, internet connections, and social media. Rwandans have embraced and adapted to new modes of communication in order to keep pace with a changing society and world.

Rwanda is something of a linguistic patchwork quilt, having four widely used languages. Kinyarwanda is the traditional language of the country and is spoken by almost everyone. French and English are also official languages. In addition, Swahili is commonly used in business and trade with members of other African countries. In spite of this mixed linguistic heritage, language has often been a unifying force rather than a divisive one.

THREE LANGUAGES

While almost everyone in Rwanda speaks Kinyarwanda, most also speak a second language. Educated Rwandans who grew up in the country are

Posters in Kigali promote the French-language newspaper *Jeune Afrique*, which means "Young Africa."

more likely to speak French as a second language. During the colonial period, French was used by the Belgians, and Belgian Catholic officials taught it in their schools. Other educated Rwandans who grew up in exile, usually in Tanzania, Kenya, or Uganda, usually learned English. Those who rely on French as a second language may know very little English, and those who rely on English, in turn, often have little knowledge of French.

The government has made three major shifts in the language of education. Before 2008, all three languages of Kinyarwanda, French, and English could be taught in schools. Most primary schools taught in Kinyarwanda up until the fourth year, when they switched to French. In 2008, the government announced that, instead, schools at every level should be taught in English. This was likely related to Rwanda's decision to cut all diplomatic ties with France at that time. However, the change was difficult to accomplish, especially since many primary school teachers did not speak English.

> ## BANTU
>
> *Bantu languages are a group within what is called the Niger-Congo language family. There are around 200 separate Bantu languages spoken by an estimated 60 million people occupying the southern third of the African continent. Both Kinyarwanda and Swahili are Bantu languages. In Rwanda, Swahili is an unofficial language, not taught in the schools but acceptable for all those who want to use it in business.*

Poor, rural communities were at a disadvantage. Teachers scrambled to learn English for the classroom, and few had appropriate English learning materials for their students. The youngest children struggled to learn an unfamiliar language that very few parents or neighbors spoke. To their relief, the government decided that early primary school could be taught in Kinyarwanda up until fourth grade, and all other grades should be taught in English. However, that decision was revoked in 2019 when it was announced, once more, that all levels of schooling should be carried out in English.

POWERFUL GESTURES

People in every culture communicate in many ways other than with words, including facial expressions, gestures, and body language. How people deal with time is also a behavior that sends messages. American businesspeople and representatives of aid agencies are frequently frustrated by the slower pace of business in Rwanda. Some come away with the feeling that a Rwandan official or businessperson is either incompetent or is trying to hide something. The truth, instead, is that business and government affairs in Rwanda are conducted at a much more relaxed pace.

Another way the treatment of time sends mixed messages is in holding meetings. Rwandans want business and government meetings to have a pleasant aspect. At the start of a meeting, for example, they prefer to spend some time exchanging pleasantries before talking business. They consider it rude to go right to the main topic. However, Americans and Europeans often show impatience with the slow pace. Rwandans interpret their facial expressions and behavior as signs that Westerners are pushy and aggressive.

Simple matters such as gestures also require interpretation. Rwandans receive gifts with both hands or with the right hand only, while touching the right elbow with the left hand. Both of these gestures are expressions of gratitude. No words of thanks are necessary. A Westerner who gives a gift and does not hear a thank you may be offended or disappointed.

MASS COMMUNICATION

Rwanda is starting to embrace instant communication. Cell phones are increasingly visible on the streets of Kigali and Huye, although they have arrived more slowly in rural areas. In 2019, there were about 9.5 million mobile phone users in Rwanda. The use of personal computers, the internet, and email is also developing. An extensive fiber-optic network has sped up progress and bypassed the more troublesome satellite connections. More than 2.6 million people, about 21 percent of the population, were internet users in 2019. This

Local, national, and international headlines make their way to the streets of Kigali.

LANGUAGES OF RWANDA

Words in Kinyarwanda and Swahili are spelled phonetically, so every letter is pronounced. If a letter is written twice, it is pronounced twice—that is, it becomes two syllables. For instance, mzee, *meaning "respected elder," is pronounced m-ZEE-ee. Also, in both languages, the stress is usually on the second-to-last syllable.*

Try pronouncing some words and phrases in the languages of Rwanda:

English	French	Kinyarwanda	Swahili
hello	bonjour	muraho	salama
goodbye	au revoir	muramukeho	kwa heri
How are you?	Comment allez-vous?	Amakura?/Bitese?	Hujambo?
I'm fine	ça va bien	amakuru/meza	sijambo
please	s'il vous plait	mubishoboye	tafadhali
thank you	merci	murakoze	asante
What's your name?	Quel est votre nom?	Witwande?	Jina lakonani?
now	maintenant	ubu/nonaha	sasa
soon	bientôt	vuba	sasa hivi
today	aujord'hui	none	leo
yesterday	hier	ejo hashize	jana
tomorrow	demain	ejo hazaza	kesho

was achieved despite the high cost of internet in Rwanda, where most users pay 7 percent of their income for service.

In the mass media, there are a number of radio stations that broadcast in Kinyarwanda, French, English, or Swahili. Listeners can choose from 35 national and international radio stations. Rwandan television produces some local programming, primarily news. Most television, however, is relayed from other countries, including news broadcasts from England and the United States. Currently, 13 television stations are operating.

The literacy rate—the number of people who can read and write—is just over 73 percent in Rwanda. Those who do read can pick up national newspapers. There are several published in different languages. The *New Times* is printed daily in English and shares articles online as well.

In 1999, the Kigali-Virunga Rotary Club voted to build a library to make up for the lack of books in Rwanda. Funds were raised nationally and from overseas donors, such as an organization called the American Friends of the Kigali Public Library. The Ministry of Education also financed and directed the library. Finally, the building opened its doors to the public in 2012. From an original collection of 12,000 books, the library now has more than 36,000 books and 700 e-books. The mission is to open a whole new world to young Rwandans, foster a culture of reading, and improve the country through literature and knowledge sharing.

SOCIAL MEDIA

Rwandans with internet service and mobile phones are likely to use their devices to connect to social media. Those who do follow the example of President Kagame, who interacts with countrymen and critics on several different platforms. In 2020, Kagame had more than 2 million followers on Twitter and

People can now get their news from print and digital sources, but the vast majority of Rwandans do not have internet access.

several hundred thousand on Instagram. The government capitalized on this means of quickly spreading information during the 2020 lockdowns to control COVID-19. At one point, Kagame used Instagram to livestream chats with local influencers in a move to reach more Rwandans online. For ordinary citizens, the five most-used social media options in Rwanda in 2021 are Facebook, Twitter, Pinterest, Instagram, and YouTube.

INTERNET LINKS

www.atlasobscura.com/articles/lake-kivu-rwanda
Read about Amashi, the little-used language spoken by the fishermen of Lake Kivu. You can also listen to a recording of a traditional fishing song in Amashi.

www.kplonline.org
Visit the Kigali Public Library website for a sense of the data and literary resources available in the capital.

www.newtimes.co.rw
Check out the latest headlines from Rwanda's *New Times* daily newspaper.

rnud.org
The Rwandan National Union for the Deaf (RNUD) advocates for the greater inclusion of deaf citizens in Rwandan society and politics.

ARTS

Women participate in a traditional dance while
wearing mushanana, a traditional garment made
from one large piece of fabric that is draped
around the waist and over one shoulder.

10

T RADITIONAL RWANDAN CRAFTS IN combination with a powerful cultural, creative drive have shaken up Rwanda's art world in the past few decades. Some individuals have turned to expressive arts to heal the pain of cultural conflict and loss, while others have kept their heritage alive with traditional crafts. Meanwhile, young makers and entrepreneurs are pouring their energy into establishing a thriving creative industry in Rwanda.

Rwanda's culture is rich and varied. This artistic tapestry includes music, dance, folktales, poetry, painting, and a wide variety of handicrafts. Artistic expression is part of daily life. On any given day, a visitor to a rural village might hear the pulsating rhythm of a half dozen *tambourinaires* (drummers), watch a Twa master potter fashion a miniature water buffalo, or listen to fieldworkers repeat an ancient chant as they work.

For a number of years, especially during the chaotic early 1990s, the arts were neglected. However, they have experienced a lively revival since 1995. Observers notice a renewed vigor in the songs and dances and an increased demand from other countries for Rwandan crafts and fine arts. The government is helping by encouraging activities that involve art, crafts, and folklore, while also economically supporting local artisans through "Made in Rwanda" initiatives.

LITERATURE

Until the Europeans arrived in the 19th century, there was no written language used in Rwanda. Instead, all three ethnic groups developed a strong oral tradition made up of poems, songs, proverbs, and chants. These oral forms are still cherished today, long after the introduction of writing in Kinyarwanda, French, and English. Storytelling and the reciting of poetry continue to be popular, and skill in any form of public speaking is admired.

In Rwanda's preliterate society, oral tradition provided a form of entertainment as well as a means of transmitting such information as history and moral lessons from generation to generation. The court of the mwami became a training place for young nobles to learn various literary forms, especially poems and songs that dealt with courage in battle. The Tutsi favored folklore dealing with the magnificence of their cattle, while the Twa composed poems and songs about their hunting skills.

One of modern Rwanda's greatest writers was Alexis Kagame. He was a man of broad intellectual achievements. Trained for the clergy, he was also a philosopher, ethnologist, and historian. Kagame wrote about Rwanda's oral

A film adaptation of Scholastique Mukasonga's book Our Lady of the Nile was released in 2020.

history and edited several volumes of the country's poetry, mythology, and folktales.

J. Saverio Naigiziki is considered another literary pioneer in Rwanda. He gained fame for his autobiography *Escapade rwandaise* (*Rwandan Adventure*) in 1949. He also wrote a critically acclaimed novel, *L'Optimiste* (*The Optimist*), in 1954 that deals with the marriage of a Hutu man and a Tutsi woman.

Many modern writers have written in fiction and nonfiction about the events of the civil war and genocide in Rwanda. Most works are autobiographical and have gained a large readership internationally. Scholastique Mukasonga is an award-winning writer who has explored life in Rwanda through fiction. Mukasonga lived in the country until the early 1990s, when she took refuge in Burundi and then France. She lost 27 of her family members, including her mother, during the genocide. Two of Mukasonga's novels about Rwanda, *Our Lady of the Nile* and *Igifu*, were published in French but have also been translated to English.

Drummers play a vital role in *intore* dances, beating out a steady rhythm that drives the movement.

SONG AND DANCE

The cultural life of Rwanda is based in tradition, with each artistic form dating back several hundred years. Music and dance are probably the most important of these forms, and both are woven into the fabric of people's daily lives. In addition to highly polished professional presentations, singing and dancing are built into ceremonies involving birth, marriage, death, the harvest, and hunting. Some special songs, called "cow songs," are created especially for herders to sing to their cattle.

On the professional level, the splendidly attired *intore* dancers, all male, are world renowned, and the intore dance troupe has toured in many countries. The intore, meaning "the chosen ones," were formed several centuries ago to perform exclusively at the royal court. Today, performances are arranged by the Enthnographic Museum in Huye.

The intore dances have changed in modern times. In the past, intore performances were usually built around warlike themes. The dances had names like *umeheto* (the bow), *ingabo* (shield), and *ikuma* (the lance), and the men carried real weapons. Over the past century, the weapons have been replaced with replicas, and the dances now emphasize movement and rhythm rather than warfare.

The intore dancers were traditionally divided into two groups. One group, called the Indashyikirwa ("the unsurpassables"), were all Tutsi. The second group, the Iishyaka ("those who challenge through their effort"), were Twa dancers led by Tutsi.

The drama and power of the dance is heightened by a drum ensemble, usually containing seven to nine drums, which provides a strong, almost hypnotic set of complex rhythms. Melodic interludes are provided by the *lulunga*, a harplike instrument with eight strings.

The costumes consist of either a short skirt or a leopard skin wrapped around the legs. Crossed straps decorated with beads are worn across the chest, and a fringe of white colobus monkey fur is worn on the head. The total effect of the tall dancers, the movement, the music, and the costumes is one of power combined with grace.

Rwandans also create more modern music. In churches throughout the country, for example, devotional singing, with strong harmonies and an upbeat tone, can be heard. Young artists can also pursue their musical interests more officially. The Nyundo Music School is a government-funded institution that aims to train professional musicians and develop Rwanda's music industry.

Before the upheaval of the 1990s, there were a number of bands and singers creating popular music, ranging from folk tunes to rock. During the 1990s, many performers fled to Europe, especially Paris and Brussels (in Belgium). Bands with names like Imena, Les Fellows, Impala, and Abamarungu combined music from different parts of Africa, especially the Democratic Republic of the Congo, with Caribbean reggae and American rock. The music is colorful, lively, and popular in Rwanda. Important artists in this style include Aimé Murefu, a guitarist who borrows from American guitarists, such as Jimi Hendrix and B. B. King.

Rock, R&B, jazz, hip-hop, rap, Afropop, and other styles of music have attracted musicians and listeners in Rwanda. Some of today's most celebrated artists in a variety of genres include Cyprien Kagorara, Knowless, Kamichi, Mani Martin, Urban Boyz, Tom Close, Miss Jojo, Riderman, Miss Shanel, Angell Mutoni, and Deo Munyakazi.

A jazz musician named Somi is part of the Rwandan diaspora, or the Rwandans who have found homes around the world. Somi was born in the United States to immigrant parents from Rwanda and Burundi. She has a strong sense of Rwandan heritage, and her musical style pays tribute to her East African roots. In November 2020, Somi made headlines with a Grammy Award nomination for her album *Holy Room*.

HANDCRAFTS

The people of Rwanda produce an amazing variety of handcrafts (also called handicrafts) that display the artisans' great skill, including weavings, ceramics, paintings, jewelry, wood carvings, ironwork, and gourd containers. Over the centuries, each craft has become highly specialized, and artisans pass on

Textile crafts based in traditional skills, like weaving and embroidery, are flourishing in Rwanda.

In the town of Nyakarimbi, near the border with Tanzania, a group of artisans carries on a tradition of decorating houses with cow-dung paintings. These paintings do indeed make use of cow dung, mixed with ash and clay. The surface is then painted in red, white, yellow, and black, using natural dyes from clay, ochre, the sap of the aloe plant, and burned banana skins.

A women's group called the Kakira Association, formed in 1995, revived the centuries-old tradition and expanded it. With natural materials, they produce the colored tiles and panels called imigongo. The art is quite beautiful with intricate geometric patterns. Following their lead, other cooperatives and artists have taken up the art form. Imigongo can now be found around Rwanda adorning traditional huts, on the walls of high-end hotels, and for sale in boutique shops and art studios.

Weaving techniques to create baskets and mats have been passed down for generations in Rwanda.

their skills, usually to a son or daughter. It would be difficult for an amateur weaver or potter to practice a craft without training by a skilled artisan.

WOVEN ART

Weaving is done almost exclusively by women. They use several different fibers, including grasses, papyrus, and banana leaves, for weaving baskets and mats. Striking geometric patterns are woven in red, black, and white. Having a collection of baskets is regarded as a sign of status.

Women also weave smaller household items, such as pot holders and table mats, usually using banana leaves. They also weave small coils that are placed on a woman's head to help support large jugs and other objects. The weavings, which include hammocks and wall hangings as well as baskets of many sizes and designs, are sold at roadside stands and in the shops of craft cooperatives in cities.

An unusual approach to weaving is seen in the Kuba cloth made in villages near Rwanda's border with the Democratic Republic of the Congo. Men make the basic cloth, weaving the central fibers of the palm leaf, and women then add an embroidered motif, creating a velvet-like fabric with an attractive geometric design. Long, horizontal shapes are intended to be wrapped around the hips and worn as a skirt. In the past, small pieces of Kuba cloth were used as currency, but that practice died out around 1900.

CARVING

Most wood carving is done by men. In many families, the wife is a weaver and the husband is a wood carver or sculptor. They make a variety of products, including bowls and jugs, tobacco pipes, stools, knife handles, and figurines. Men also make drums and other musical instruments.

Bamboo grows naturally in Rwanda's high-elevation forests and can be fashioned into a wide variety of furniture and crafts.

CERAMICS

Centuries ago, the Twa were hunters and gatherers living in the mountainside forests of Central Africa. As more and more people moved into the regions and the forests were cleared for agriculture and pastureland, the Twa moved into the valleys. There they taught themselves to be outstanding potters without having access to special tools or the knowledge of kilns for firing their ceramics. They also developed great skill as dancers and became favored entertainers at the royal court. They sang and danced for the mwami and his family and made their pottery.

Twa potters gather clay from marshes in low valleys. They stomp the clay with their feet to soften it, then shape it with their hands. Their pottery is plain but sturdy and attractive. They make a variety of objects, including vases, flowerpots, cooking pots, stoves, candleholders, and all sorts of small figures of Rwanda's animals. The Twa fire their ceramics in a hole in the ground, covering the objects with a hot fire made from grasses and twigs, topped with a layer of earth.

CREATIVE COMMUNITY

Until recently, the lack of sales outlets had severely limited the earnings of artisans. Many men and women tried to sell their wares at roadside stands, where the items were often damaged by rain or road dust. Apart from market stalls in Kigali and other towns, there was no way to reach a larger public, especially tourists.

Since 2000, government agencies, international organizations, and young entrepreneurs have expanded the crafts market. Several government offices have displays of not only pottery, weavings, and carvings, but also of paintings, jewelry, and ironwork. Sales stalls have been established at airports, at travel offices, and in some hotels. Rwanda's embassies and consulates are also promoting the country's crafts.

New and trendy galleries have become a fixture of Rwanda's cities, especially Kigali. Inema Art Center in the capital showcases and supports the work of local and international talents. Inema was founded in 2012 by two artists and brothers, Innocent Nkurunziza and Emmanuel Nkuranga, with the goal of expanding creative arts in Rwanda. Since then, it has become a major gallery, not only in Rwanda, but also for the region of East Africa. Many of Rwanda's emerging artists have ties to the center.

Ivuka Arts is a second major art studio in Kigali. It was founded in 2007 by the artist Colin Sekajugo in order to nurture artists and connect the people of Rwanda with transformative art. Inema Art Center, Ivuka Arts, and the young generation of artists they've fostered have helped to establish the identity of Rwandan art and artists. The creative community in Rwanda also includes fashion designers, dancers, models, filmmakers, and more.

PUBLIC ART

Rwandans do not have to go to a gallery to see art. Public art has been cropping up in Rwanda's cities with increasing frequency thanks to a group called Kurema Kureba Kwiga, which means "to create, to see, to learn" in English. Founded in 2013, Kurema brings whimsical or thought-provoking visual stories to the streets. Movement and color are features of these works, which often include portraits or geometric designs. Many murals convey powerful social messages of conservation, unity, and equality, while others are more playful. Kurema has partnered with the government and various businesses to bring vivid, site-specific murals to places around Rwanda.

During the COVID-19 pandemic, the government commissioned Kurema and 14 artists to spread awareness of public health measures. The artists created a series of large murals around Kigali with a range of subjects like handwashing, mask wearing, and social distancing. The muralists, including artists Innocent Kagabo and Bonfils Ngabonziza, hoped to inspire people to adopt healthy behaviors in the spirit of collective action. By commissioning these murals, the government hopes to optimize the influence of the creative arts in Rwanda.

This brightly colored mural in Kigali was created by Kurema Kureba Kwiga to raise awareness about HIV/AIDS.

INTERNET LINKS

berkleycenter.georgetown.edu/interviews/a-discussion-with-eric-ngangare-poet-singer-and-storyteller-rwanda
This interview with Eric Ngangare, a spoken word poet, musician, and performer who goes by the stage name 1Key, explores his personal story and relationship with Rwanda.

www.inemaartcenter.com
The website for the Inema Art Center in Kigali showcases the work of Rwandan artists.

www.somimusic.com
Visit the website of Rwandan-American jazz singer Somi, where you can listen to samples of her unique vocal style.

www.youtube.com/watch?v=cDKg0Rs8KbI
Watch spoken word artist Naleli Rugengi perform at a Spoken Word Rwanda event.

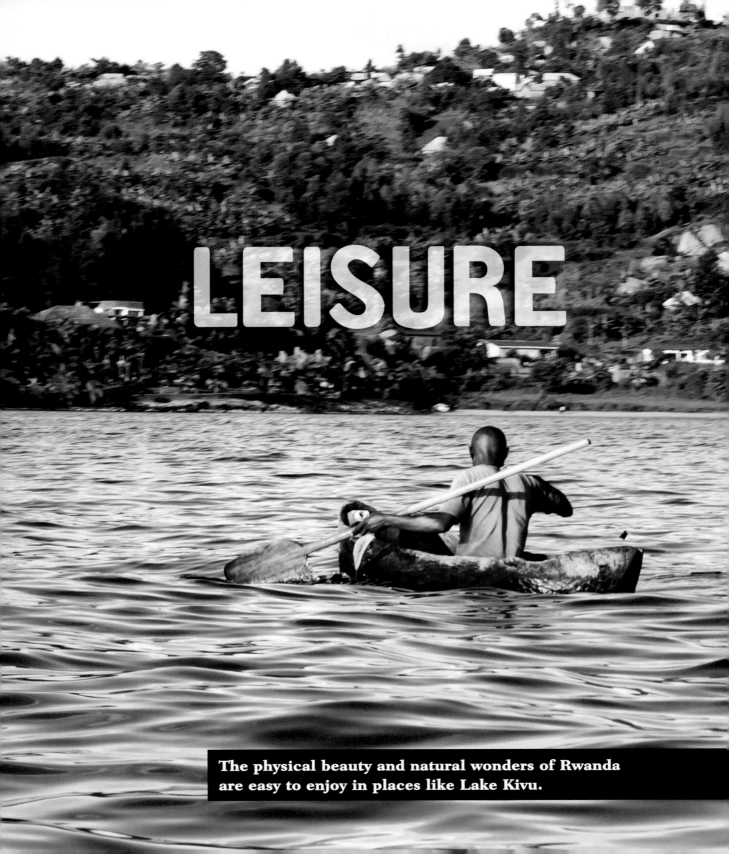

LEISURE

The physical beauty and natural wonders of Rwanda are easy to enjoy in places like Lake Kivu.

11

THE ATTRACTIONS THAT DRAW tourists to Rwanda are often very different from the places and everyday activities that bring pleasure to locals. Rwanda is a small, easily traveled country with beautiful scenery, and it offers an appealing variety of wildlife. However, the vast majority of visitors to the stunning national parks come from outside of the country. Many young people in training to become workers and guides in the national parks and forests have discovered the fun and excitement of wildlife safaris and trekking for primates. However, few of Rwanda's ordinary citizens could afford the expensive permits required to view mountain gorillas in their natural habitat.

Leisure activities have been limited by the fact that nearly three-quarters of people live by farming or herding, and most of them have little time or money for leisure pursuits. Access to electricity is also spotty. Few Rwandans can spend an evening watching television, and other entertainments, such as internet, streaming services, and video games, are rare. Nor do the vast majority of people have the opportunity to engage in organized activities, such as team sports, clubs, or activities, which require expensive equipment.

In spite of the limitations, Rwandans do have fun. A variety of activities are accessible to almost everyone, including parties, family events, pickup soccer games, and a growing number of spectator sports. Television is limited, but many people have radios that give them an important connection with the rest of the country and world. Music blares from storefronts, cafés, and pickup trucks, and Rwandans come together in public spaces to enjoy conversations with strangers and friends.

EVERYDAY ENJOYMENTS

The majority of Rwandans work hard from first light to dark, herding sheep or goats, tending to crops, or creating crafts to sell. Children, too, work hard,

A trip to the beaches of Lake Kivu can be a welcome change of pace for farmers and fishers, though few Rwandans are taught to swim.

carrying the day's supply of water or collecting enough firewood for cooking and heat. After the evening meal, people do not have much time or energy for leisure pursuits.

A culture of reading is fairly new in Rwanda, and access to television is limited to people living in the few urban centers. However, the country's oral tradition provides many families with an extensive "library" of poems, songs, riddles, folktales, proverbs, jokes, and games. Evenings spent around the glowing embers of a fire or the light of a kerosene lamp are likely to involve an elder telling stories or reciting poems or an entire family singing.

Family gatherings provide more extended periods for enjoyment. Birthdays, weddings, naming parties, and holidays are filled with eating, playing games, and solving riddles or puzzles. Most noticeable at these occasions is the Rwandan love of music and dance. People of all ages can spend hours in fast-paced dances, often with the accompaniment of a single drum.

Rwandan children love playing games. Many are simple outdoor games, variations on such familiar contests as tag or hide-and-seek. Indoor games are equally popular, especially board games. The "board" is usually handmade,

Igisoro is a two-player game that requires a wooden board with rows of bowls, or pits, and 64 seeds. Each player moves the seeds around the board, passing them from pit to pit.

Children in Rwanda use games and toys made from simple materials to entertain themselves.

and the game pieces are seeds or pebbles. Some games are even simpler, like one that involves tossing a half-dozen seeds into the air and catching as many as possible on the back of one's hand. Some board games, such as mancala and *igisoro*, have become popular in other countries and are now commercially produced.

Radio is a popular source of entertainment for diverse groups of people in the city and country. Dramatic radio plays harness the power of oral storytelling and reach listeners throughout Rwanda. A popular children's radio show called *Itetero* has aired weekly on Radio Rwanda since 2015. The show is a collaboration between the Rwanda Broadcasting Agency (RBA), the Imbuto Foundation, and UNICEF aimed at providing quality programming for young Rwandans. The name *Itetero* is Kinyarwandan for "children's nurturing space." The show features stories and sketches acted out by children for children. Common themes promote cultural values and are carefully designed to support child development and learning. In some rural areas, families with young children gather to listen to the show and participate in activities together. Since it began, *Itetero* has had a big impact for children, families, and communities around Rwanda. It is a program that encourages community-building while being both educational and fun.

URBAN OPTIONS

Educated families in Rwanda, especially those with incomes well above the poverty line, have greater possibilities for leisure activities. While Rwanda has very few wealthy people, it does have a growing middle class. People who work in such fields as health care, government, business, banking, and education engage in activities more like those of Americans or Europeans.

Television is gradually becoming available, for example, at least in such urban centers as Kigali and Huye, although Rwanda has fewer TV sets per capita than any other country in Africa. The country also ranks low in per capita personal computers, and only 21.7 percent of the population are internet subscribers.

Movies are also offering new entertainment possibilities. A movie theater was opened in the Kigali Business Center in 2001. It shows international and independent films, one in the afternoon and another in the evening. Most of the films are in English, with subtitles in French. The addition of children's programs and the Planet Cinema Restaurant has turned the Business Center into an evening and weekend destination for family entertainment.

Kigali, by far the largest city, offers a few additional entertainment facilities. The French-Rwandan cultural exchange arranges films, plays, and performances in music and dance. The tourist board also promotes Twa dance performances and visits to their pottery studios. The lively and colorful dances, sometimes humorous and often dramatic, last more than two hours and are now becoming popular with Rwandan audiences, especially children.

A number of performing arts and theater companies provide entertainment in Rwanda's larger cities. Tickets to see Rwanda's National Ballet offer an experience different from other ballet performances around the world as the company incorporates traditional folk dance into its choreography. The Impala Orchestra likewise has distinct ties to Rwandan heritage that accompany its modern musical selections. For those outside Kigali, the Mashirika Performing Arts and Theatre Company has engaged communities around Rwanda with dramatic presentations and radio plays since it was founded in 1997.

Shopping is a favorite form of entertainment, especially on market days (usually Friday and Sundays). Several streets in Kigali and Huye are lined with shops, some selling local crafts and others a variety of European, African, and Indian wares. The markets are even more popular, drawing large, colorful, and noisy crowds. Open-air stalls are piled high with fresh foods, clothing, furniture, and housewares.

A growing number of middle-class Rwandans enjoy their evenings at restaurants, bars, and clubs, where they mix with Europeans and Americans working with businesses or international agencies. Some establishments rely

TOUR DU RWANDA

Billed as the biggest sporting event in the country, the Tour du Rwanda captures the attention of an estimated 3 million spectators each year. For one week, cyclists from around the world are immersed in the gloriously hilly landscape of Rwanda while competing. The 2020 race covered 552 miles (889 km) over the course of the week. Rwandans enjoy the free entertainment, turning out around the country to see the parade of athletes whiz by.

Tour du Rwanda is organized by the Rwanda Cycling Federation. The first race took place in 1988, but it was unable to continue through most of the 1990s. The event has been held annually ever since resuming in 2001.

The Tour du Rwanda passes through many cities and villages in Rwanda, including Muhanga, where this photograph was taken.

on DJs, but many have live bands playing African, European, and American music. Many Rwandans prefer eating at one of the quiet courtyard restaurants, tucked away from the bustling shopping areas. These moderately priced

restaurants serve a variety of cuisines, including Chinese, Ethiopian, Indian, and Italian.

SPORTING EVENTS

On a Saturday or Sunday afternoon, cars, minibuses, and pedestrians fill the roads leading to Kisimenti crossroads on the outskirts of Kigali. Their destination is the Amahoro Stadium, where all major soccer (called football in Rwanda) matches are played. For a long time, the Amahoro experience was not much like a sports event in the United States. There was no scoreboard and no program listing the players. Children sold tickets outside, and the match started more or less on time. Still, the game itself unfolded like soccer

Though most soccer enthusiasts flock to the stadium or park to enjoy the game, these entrepreneurs in Kigali get serious about table-top soccer.

games everywhere, packed with suspense and excitement. Rwanda's national team plays very well, and many of the local club teams have developed into strong competitors. In October 2003, only nine years after the genocide, the national team qualified for the 2004 Africa Cup of Nations. The team, known as Amavubi, or "Wasps," stung two more experienced teams—the Uganda Cranes and the Ghana Black Stars—to qualify.

When the Rwandan national team beat the Cranes, the Ugandans could not believe that their smaller, war-ravaged neighbor could win. They cried foul, claiming that the Rwandans had won through witchcraft by putting the remains of a chicken in the Ugandan goalmouth so that the Ugandan team could not score. Rwanda won 1—0.

Although Rwanda did not win the cup, simply qualifying in a competition involving 52 African nations was a great morale booster for the country and created a great surge of enthusiasm for soccer as well as other sports. Rwandans continue to cheer on their team for another chance at the Africa Cup of Nations, and they're hopeful for a shot at the World Cup one day.

Since the late 1990s, more and more secondary schools have developed soccer programs, and local communities have organized club teams. Other sports are also becoming popular. The Cercle Sportif, for example, located in Lower Kiyovu, has facilities for tennis, volleyball, basketball, swimming, and even badminton. Cycling, including mountain biking, is gaining popularity, and even golf is now available at the Nyarutarama Golf Club.

Although none of these trends, except for the enthusiasm for soccer, is anything like a mass movement, the new interests are signs of Rwanda's progress. Each year, more families find they have the free time and extra income to enjoy leisure activities. In addition, television, the internet, and schools are making young people more aware of the possibilities, ranging from basketball to in-line skating.

CRICKET

One of the most surprising sports played in Rwanda is cricket. Most countries that play the game have had a long association with Great Britain, such as India, Kenya, and Tanzania, which were all once British colonies. Rwanda did not have such an experience, but cricket is thriving. It became popular after the genocide, when Rwandans who had been living in exile in Uganda, Tanzania, and Kenya returned with a passion for the sport.

The Rwanda Cricket Association (RCA) lists several teams in Kigali and Huye, including some that represent foreign nationals living in Rwanda, like the British Community Team and three teams from the Asian community. Around 5,000 people play through the RCA.

Matches are held throughout the year at the Gahanga Cricket Stadium outside Kigali, which opened in 2017. Locals call the stadium the "Lords of Africa." The wicket, a term for the cricket field, meets the standards of the International Cricket Council.

Rwanda hopes to popularize cricket in schools as a sport for boys and girls. The RCA organizes tournaments at primary and secondary schools. The game has also recently become more popular among university students. Women have been encouraged to take up the sport, despite its traditional appeal to men.

INTERNET LINKS

mashirika.com/about-us
Learn more about the dramatic offerings of the Mashirika Performing Arts and Media Company on their website.

rwandacricket.weebly.com
Follow the latest developments in the world of cricket on this website from the Rwanda Cricket Association.

www.tourdurwanda.rw
The Tour du Rwanda website details the route and requirements of the yearly cycling race.

FESTIVALS

Rwandan dancers take part in Africa Day, a holiday on May 25 that fosters unity among African nations.

12

SECULAR AND RELIGIOUS celebrations mark the passage of time and the commemoration of important events in Rwanda. The country observes national holidays, and individual citizens honor additional occasions based on their religion or local community. Religious festivals are celebrated by Protestant, Roman Catholic, and Muslim Rwandans in ways that often overlap. Many of these holidays also contain elements or lore derived from traditional tribal practices.

Some holidays have both secular and religious qualities. For example, New Year's Eve and New Year's Day are times for parties, dances, and lots of food. Roman Catholics also go to Mass, and several Protestant churches have services. Peace and National Unity Day on July 4 is a time to celebrate the end of the mass killings in 1994. It is also a time for solemn remembrance of the nearly one million people who perished.

A number of religious holidays follow a lunar calendar, which is based on the phases of the moon. Nearly all Muslim holidays are scheduled according to the lunar calendar. Every year, a holiday falls about 11 days earlier than it did the year before. Some Christian holidays, such as Easter, are also scheduled according to the lunar calendar.

CHRISTIAN TRADITIONS

The inclusion of traditional tribal dances and festivities with Christian holidays is a sign of the syncretic, or mixed, nature of religion in Rwanda.

There is a good deal of variety in the way different Christian churches celebrate holidays. This is true of Roman Catholic churches as well as Protestant because some Catholic churches have rather loose ties with the official Church. One reason for the variation is that many churches incorporate traditional tribal practices into their celebrations. At some holiday festivals, it is not unusual to have tribal drums or intore dancers as part of a celebration of Christmas or All Saints' Day.

While nearly all churches, Catholic as well as Protestant, include at least some traditional tribal beliefs or practices, the extent varies from church to church. Some observers say that in many Protestant churches the festivals and services are more tribal than standard Protestant. In fact, some authorities say that as many as one-third of Rwandans should be classified as followers of indigenous (traditional) religions. When a Christian church celebrates All Saints' Day (November 1), for example, many in the congregation are likely to think of the Christian saints as bazimu, the spirits of the dead who reside in Ikuzimu (the underworld). Similarly, the Feast of the Ascension in May, the 40th day after Easter, which is celebrated by both Protestants and Catholics and marks the ascension of Jesus into Heaven, may be seen by many as a journey by Imana, the supreme being.

How much of traditional practice and belief enters into a particular church can often depend on the particular minister or priest. Some are willing to let the congregants maintain many of their ancient practices in order to keep them as members of the church. This is particularly true of some evangelical churches. Often led by charismatic preachers, these churches have won thousands of converts in the past, often by holding festivals consisting almost entirely of tribal music, songs, and dances.

Ministers and priests are also frequently invited to participate in tribal festivals that have been held for many centuries. Springtime, for example,

New Year's Day. . . . . . . January 1
Easter Week . . . . March/April
Ascension Thursday . . . . . May
Feast of the Assumption . . . August 15
All Saints' Day . . . . November 1
Christmas . . . . December 25

is a time of renewal and planting, and every village celebrates with prayers, music, dances, processions, and special foods. Catholic or Protestant leaders easily fit their prayers and sermons into the other activities. Much the same occurs in the late summer, when the harvest festival is held on August 1. A number of villages also celebrate the harvest at other times, depending on when local crops are ready.

ISLAMIC HOLIDAYS

Somewhere between 2 and 10 percent of Rwandans are Muslim. Most Muslims live in Kigali and nearby towns. The most important period for Muslims is the month of Ramadan, which falls in the ninth month of the lunar calendar. During this 30-day period, the faithful observe a very strict fast each day from first light until dusk. After dark, they break the fast with a big family meal.

Following Ramadan, the first two or three days in the month of Shawwal are the time for a joyous festival called Eid al-Fitr, meaning the Feast of the Fast Breaking. Muslims gather with family and friends for feasts, prayers, and the exchanging of gifts.

Other important Muslim holy days include Eid al-Adha, which commemorates the moment when Abraham, about to sacrifice his son Ishmael to show obedience to God, is told not to harm the boy. This event is also commemorated in Judaism and Christianity. For Muslims, the holy day coincides with the end of the hajj, the pilgrimage to Mecca. Another important day is Mawlid, the birthday of the Prophet Muhammad.

SECULAR HOLIDAYS

The important national holidays are connected with independence and the restoration of peace in Rwanda after the genocide. National Day, July 1, celebrates achieving independence from Belgium in 1962 and the creation of the republic. Traditionally, this is a day for parades, a review of the army, and speeches delivered by the president and other dignitaries, including representatives of Belgium's government.

Armed Services Day on October 26 has been a similar occasion. The government has felt it important to continue to display the power of Rwanda's military, not only out of pride for how swiftly the RPF's army ended the genocide, but also as a warning to Hutu rebels living in the Democratic Republic of the Congo or Burundi that Rwanda can handle any insurgency. Rwanda, however, has benefited from large sums of foreign aid, and some of the country's major financial supporters expressed concern at the amount of resources devoted to military spending in the past. In response, the government quietly scaled back the festivities.

National Mourning Day takes place every April 7 to remember the start of the genocide in 1994. It is followed by a period of mourning that ends with Liberation Day. July 4 is Peace and National Unity Day, also known as Liberation Day. This marks the success of the 1994 invasion by the RPF, which stormed into Rwanda, liberating terrified Tutsi and Hutu moderates who were hiding from the death squads. The celebration has always been one of relief and somber thanksgiving rather than one of exuberance.

A spontaneous holiday was celebrated in 2003 after Rwanda's soccer victory over Ghana. The resulting joyous celebration was an all-night affair, and the streets of Kigali were filled with people shouting and singing, accompanied by the noise of honking car and bus horns. The celebration was held in the same week as Independence Day and Liberation Day.

President Kagame makes appearances at a number of public holidays in Rwanda and abroad. He's seen here at a celebration of Ugandan independence in the nation's capital, Kampala.

National Mourning Day is called Kwikibuka in Kinyarwanda.

Gorilla-naming ceremonies are a more recent addition to the list of state-sponsored holidays. For one week every September, a schedule of lively and colorful activities and educational events are planned alongside the primary naming ceremony. The event is called Kwita Izina, which means "to give a name." It follows the customary naming ceremonies for children, which occur when an infant is three or four months old. Mountain gorillas have never reproduced in captivity, so each birth of the endangered species in the wild is a cause for celebration. During the ceremony, each baby gorilla born in the past year is given a name that suits their personality. A growing population has been recorded for the endangered species, which is a source of pride for many Rwandans. Speeches, performances, songs, and intore dances express the participants' joy over another year of successful conservation.

Intore dancers perform for the thousands of visitors each year who flock to Kinigi for gorilla-naming ceremonies.

INTERNET LINKS

www.nationalgeographic.com/travel/destinations/africa/rwanda/partner-content-next-generation-of-gorillas/
In this article, a *National Geographic* reporter records their experience at a 2020 gorilla-naming ceremony in Rwanda.

www.newtimes.co.rw/news/ramadan-all-you-need-know-about-holy-month-fasting
Read this *New Times* article for insight into how Ramadan is observed in Rwanda.

International celebrities, like Sir David Attenborough, have taken part in gorilla-naming ceremonies.

FOOD

Most meals in Kigali are prepared simply with vegetables grown in the garden or purchased in a market.

MOST RWANDAN DISHES ARE centered around a few vegetables, grains, or proteins cooked simply. Many of the nearly three-quarters of Rwandans who are farmers grow their own food. As a result, some of the most common crops—potatoes, beans, sorghum, and bananas—make up the backbone of the Rwandan diet. Dairy from goats and cows also features heavily in local cuisine.

The foods of Rwanda are similar to those of other countries in East Africa, especially Tanzania and Kenya. People enjoy a wide variety of fresh foods, including bananas, coconuts, mangoes, oranges, and pineapples, as well as an assortment of vegetables. The most common staples served with meat or fish are rice, boiled potatoes, or chips (french fries).

The diet of rural Rwandans is quite simple. One of the most common dishes is a cornmeal mixture called *ugali*, which looks something like mashed potatoes. Ugali is eaten plain or used to make *uji*, a kind of thin porridge. The standard bread, called *chapati*, is a flatbread with a rather sweet taste. Rural people rarely eat meat, but when they do, the favorites are either goat kebabs called brochettes or a meat stew served with ugali or boiled potatoes.

Dodo is a Rwandan dish made from green amaranth or cassava leaves.

Raw ingredients, like locally milled flour, are sold at open-air markets.

CITY TASTES

People in Kigali and the larger towns generally have a more varied diet than rural Rwandans. Most urban dwellers eat meat more frequently, and they also have a variety of restaurants from which to choose. Professional people and business managers often eat at restaurants specializing in various international cuisines, such as Chinese, French, Italian, and Indian. Other urban Rwandans often prefer lower-priced restaurants, many of which serve buffet or cafeteria style. Restaurant meals built around chicken, steak, or fish are popular, with side dishes of boiled potatoes, rice, or chips. The most common fish is tilapia, a freshwater fish. Foreign visitors are often struck by the huge portions served in restaurants and the low prices.

Urban Rwandans also encounter a variety of fast foods. Some restaurants serve American-style hamburgers and pizza. Roadside stalls offer roasted corn, sodas, bottled water, and *mandazi*, which are sweet doughnuts.

Both city and rural families shop at open-air markets rather than at grocery stores or supermarkets. Fresh fruits and vegetables are displayed in open crates and baskets. Shoppers fill their shopping bags with their selections rather than picking up prepackaged goods. Meats are purchased from a butcher, with chicken, beef, and goat being the most popular.

Sambaza, small fingerling fish, are a good source of protein and are often served as starters at restaurants.

MEALS

Breakfast is usually a simple meal. Country people often have mandazi, fruit, and hot tea. In urban areas, city workers often choose French bread or croissants rather than mandazi. Rwandan tea, called *chai* in Swahili, is often made by boiling water, tea, milk, and sugar together, creating a thick, sweet, milky concoction.

The main meal is usually served at midday, but this is changing among urban Rwandans. One reason for the decreasing emphasis on the noon meal is a new government regulation shortening the lunch hour of government workers. In addition, Rwandans who dine out with foreign businesspeople or aid workers find that it is much more convenient to eat the main meal in the evening.

Whenever it is served, the largest meal of the day is likely to include a stew made with beans or meat. Side dishes, in addition to boiled potatoes or rice, might include sweet potatoes, yams, ugali or *matoke* (cooked banana or plantain), and chapati.

Some people enjoy a beer made from bananas that have been buried in the ground for several days. Other beverages include milk or fruit juice for children, while adults are likely to have wine, a local beer called Primus, bottled water, chai, or sometimes coffee. Even though Rwanda is a large exporter of coffee, it hasn't caught on as a very popular drink in the country. More Rwandans prefer tea. Those who do drink coffee may be more inclined to try African Coffee, a mix of espresso, ginger, milk, and chocolate.

Matoke is made with cooked banana or plantain and added spices.

INTERNET LINKS

www.newtimes.co.rw/section/read/94601
Read about the process for preparing matoke in this article from the *New Times*.

theculturetrip.com/africa/rwanda/articles/unique-things-for-a-foodie-to-eat-in-rwanda
This article provides an overview of the best foods to try in Kigali.

MANDAZI

Mandazi is a sweet, fried dough often available as a street food in Rwanda. It may be served plain or with toppings like Nutella or honey.

1 teaspoon active dry yeast
½ cup (118 milliliters) warm water
3 cups all-purpose flour
½ teaspoon salt
1 teaspoon cardamom
1 teaspoon cinnamon
1 tablespoon vegetable oil
1 egg
½ cup (118 mL) coconut milk
½ cup sugar
vegetable oil for frying
confectioners' sugar for dusting

Dissolve yeast in a small bowl with the warm water, and let sit for 5 minutes until frothy.

In a large bowl, mix together flour, salt, cardamom, and cinnamon. Mix together vegetable oil, egg, coconut milk, sugar, and yeast mixture separately. Add the wet ingredients into the large bowl.

Mix until the dough no longer sticks to the side of the bowl, adding extra flour if needed.

Place the dough in an oiled bowl, cover with a towel, and let rest in a warm place for 1 hour to rise.

In a deep fryer, pan, or wok, heat oil to 350°F (175°C).

Cut the dough into smaller pieces, and roll out each piece to a 0.5-inch (12.7 millimeter) thickness. Cut each piece into triangles. Fry the triangles in the hot oil on both sides until golden.

Let the fried dough drain on a paper towel before sprinkling with confectioners' sugar.

FRIED BEANS

Cooked beans are a common and simple side dish in Rwandan cuisine. They can be served alongside rice, roasted potatoes, cabbage, or meat.

2 tablespoons vegetable oil
3 onions, finely chopped
2 garlic cloves, minced
4 cups canned red kidney beans
Salt, pepper, and cayenne pepper to taste

Heat vegetable oil in a large skillet over medium-high heat.

Sauté onions and garlic in the oil about 3 to 5 minutes until the onions are soft.

Add beans and seasonings to taste. Stir, reduce heat, and simmer for 7 to 12 minutes until hot through.

A   **B**   **C**   **D**

1

N

Capital city
Major town
Mountain Peak

Feet   Meters
9,900   3,000
6,600   2,000
3,300   1,000

U G A N D A

2

**DEMOCRATIC
REPUBLIC OF
THE CONGO**

Kagitumba

Rwemhasha

Akagera

**KIBUNGO
BYUMBA**

Lubirizi
Nyagatare

Muvumba

NYAGATERE

Butaro

Kidaho

Kirambo

L. Burera

BURERA

Mulindi

Gatunda

L. Rwanyakizinga

Virunga Mts.

MUSANZE

Musanze

Busogo

Cyamba

Ngarama

Gabiro

L. Mikindi

Kora

Mutura

▲ *Mount
Karisimbi
(14,797 ft /
4,510 m)*

Byumba

Kinihirai

GATSIBO

RUBAVU

Kagali

Rubavu

NYABIHU

Kabaya

GAKENKE

Rushashi

RULINDO

Rutare

Murambi

Kinyami

GICUMBI

Muhara

L. Hugo

Ruhara

L. Kivumba

Nyundo

Ngaru

Nyabarongo

Mbogo

Shyorongi

*Lake
Muhazi*

KAYONZA

Ngororero

Kiyumba

Kinyinya

Gikoro

Rwamagara

L. Ihema

*Lake
Kivu*

NGORORERO

Runda

GASABO

KIGALI

RWAMAGANA

Kayonza

Kigarama

L. Nasho

RUTSIRO

Bulinga

NYARUGENGE

KICUKIRO

Bicumbi

*Lake
Mugesera*

Kibungo

L. Mpanga

L. Cyambwe

Mabanza

MUHANGA

Muhanga

Butamwa

KARONGI

Karongi

Birambo

KAMONYI

BUGESERA

NGOMA

KIREHE

Gishyita

Bwakira

RUHANGO

Masango

Rilima

Sare

Gashora

Rusumo

Rwamatamu

Ruhango

NYANZA

Gatagara

Ngenda

Nemba

Bare

Kirehe

Kaduha

Nyabisindu

*Lake
Cyohoha
Sud*

*Lake
Rweru*

NYAMASHEKE

Rwesero

Gisakura

NYAMAGABE

Karaba

Rusatira

TANZANIA

Kamembe

Rusizi

Rwumba

Nyamagabe

Karama

Akagera

Karengera

Kitabi

HUYE

Gisagara

RUSIZI

Bugumya

Ruramba

Huye

GISAGARA

Cyimbogo

Ruzizi

Bugarama

NYARUGURU

Busoro

Munini

Akanyaru

Runyombyi

5

B U R U N D I

MAP OF RWANDA

Birambo, B3
Bugarama, A4
Bugumya, A4
Bulinga, B3
Busogo, B2
Busoro, B4
Butamwa, C3
Bwakira, B3
Byumba, C2

Cyamba, C2
Cyimbogo, A4

Gabiro, C2
Gashora, C3
Gatagara, B4
Gatunda, C2
Gicumbi, C3
Gikoro, C3
Gisagara, B4
Gisakura, A4
Gishyita, B3

Huye (Butare), B4

Kabaya, B3
Kaduha, B4
Kagali, B2
Kagitumba, C2
Kamembe, A4
Karaba, B4
Karama, B4
Karengera, A4
Karongi (Kibuye), B3
Kayonza, C3
Kibungo, C3, D3
Kigali, C3

Kigarama, D3
Kinihirai, C2
Kinyami, C3
Kinyinya, C3
Kirambo, B2
Kitabi, B4
Kiyumba, B3
Kora, B2

Lake Burera, B2
Lake Cyambwe, D3
Lake Cyohoha Sud, C4
Lake Ihema, D3
Lake Kivu, A2—A4, B3
Lake Kivumba, D3
Lake Mikindi, D2
Lake Mpanga, D3
Lake Mugesera, C3
Lake Muhazi, C3
Lake Nasho, D3
Lake Ruhondo, B2
Lake Rwanyakizinga, D2
Lake Rweru, C4
Lubirizi, C2

Mabanza, B3
Masango, B3
Mbogo, C3
Mount Karisimbi, B2
Muhanga (Gitarama), B3
Muhara, C3
Mulindi, C2

Munini, B4
Murambi, C3
Musanze (Ruhengeri), B2
Mutura, B2
Muvumba, C2

Nemba, C4
Ngarama, C2
Ngaru, B3
Ngenda, C4
Ngororero, B3
Nyabisindu, B4
Nyagatare, C2
Nyamagabe (Gikongoro), B4
Nyundo, B3

Rilima, C3
Rubavu (Gisenyi), B3
Ruhango, B3
Ruhara, C3
Runda, C3
Runyombyi, B4
Ruramba, B4
Rusatira, B4

Rushashi, B3
Rusizi (Cyangugu), A4
Rutare, C3
Rwamagara, C3
Rwamatamu, A3
Rwemhasha, C2
Rwesero, A4
Rwumba, A4

Sare, C3
Shyorongi, C3

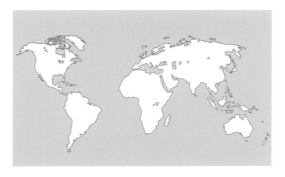

ECONOMIC RWANDA

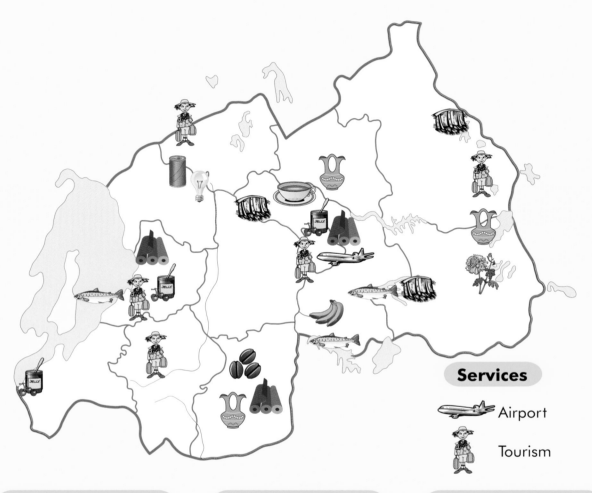

Services

 Airport

 Tourism

Manufacturing

 Food Products

 Handicrafts

 Textiles

Agriculture

 Bananas

Chrysanthemums

 Coffee

 Tea

Natural Resources

Fish

 Hydroelectricity

Tin Ore

 Tungsten Ore

ABOUT THE ECONOMY

All figures are 2017 estimates unless otherwise noted.

GROSS DOMESTIC PRODUCT (GDP)
$24.68 billion

PER CAPITA GDP
$2,100

GDP GROWTH RATE
6.1 percent

GDP BY SECTOR
agriculture 30.9 percent; industry 17.6 percent; services 51.5 percent

LAND AREA
10,169 square miles (26,338 sq km)

AGRICULTURAL PRODUCTS
coffee, tea, bananas, pyrethrum, beans, sorghum, potatoes

NATURAL RESOURCES
gold, tungsten ore (wolframite), tin ore (cassiterite), methane, hydroelectric power, arable land

CURRENCY
Rwandan Franc (RWF)
USD 1 = 971 RWF (2021)

INDUSTRIES
agricultural products, shoes, soap, furniture, textiles, cement, small-scale beverages, plastic goods, cigarettes

MAJOR EXPORTS
coffee, tea, pyrethrum, tin ore, hides

EXPORT PARTNERS
United Arab Emirates, Kenya, Switzerland, Democratic Republic of the Congo, United States, Singapore

MAJOR IMPORTS
foodstuffs, machinery, steel, petroleum products, construction materials

IMPORT PARTNERS
China, Uganda, India, Kenya, Tanzania, United Arab Emirates

LEADING FOREIGN INVESTORS
Belgium, France, Germany, Great Britain

INFLATION RATE
3.3 percent (2019)

POPULATION BELOW THE INTERNATIONAL POVERTY LINE
43 percent (2019)

CULTURAL RWANDA

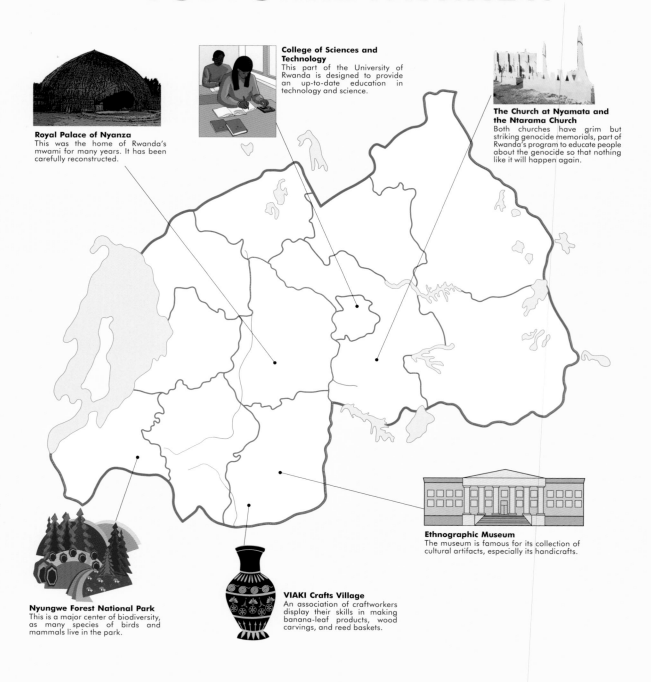

Royal Palace of Nyanza
This was the home of Rwanda's mwami for many years. It has been carefully reconstructed.

College of Sciences and Technology
This part of the University of Rwanda is designed to provide an up-to-date education in technology and science.

The Church at Nyamata and the Ntarama Church
Both churches have grim but striking genocide memorials, part of Rwanda's program to educate people about the genocide so that nothing like it will happen again.

Ethnographic Museum
The museum is famous for its collection of cultural artifacts, especially its handicrafts.

Nyungwe Forest National Park
This is a major center of biodiversity, as many species of birds and mammals live in the park.

VIAKI Crafts Village
An association of craftworkers display their skills in making banana-leaf products, wood carvings, and reed baskets.

ABOUT THE CULTURE

All figures are 2017 estimates unless otherwise noted.

OFFICIAL NAME
Republic of Rwanda

NATIONAL FLAG
three horizontal bands of sky blue, yellow, and green, plus a golden sun with 24 rays in the top right-hand corner; the flag has no red; the artist chose instead "the colors of peace"

NATIONAL ANTHEM
"Rwanda Nziza" ("Beautiful Rwanda")

CAPITAL
Kigali

OTHER MAJOR CITIES
Huye (formerly Butare)

POPULATION
12,712,431 (2020)

URBAN POPULATION
17.4 percent

POPULATION DENSITY
1,249 per square mile (482 per sq km)

ETHNIC GROUPS
Hutu 84 percent, Tutsi 15 percent, Twa 1 percent (estimated)

RELIGIOUS GROUPS
Protestant 49.5 percent; Roman Catholic 43.7 percent; Muslim 2 percent

TIME
Greenwich Mean Time (GMT) plus 2 hours

LIFE EXPECTANCY
male: 63 years; female: 67 years

OFFICIAL LANGUAGES
Kinyarwanda, French, English

EDUCATION
free and compulsory for ages 7 to 12

LITERACY RATE
male: 77.6 percent; female 69.4 percent

NATIONAL HOLIDAYS
New Year's Day (January 1), Democracy Day (January 28), National Day of Mourning (April 7), Labor Day (May 1), National Day (July 1), Peace and Unity Day (July 4), Armed Forces Day (October 26)

FAMOUS RWANDANS
Paul Kagame—military leader who led the 1994 RPF invasion that ended the genocide; elected fifth president in April 2000; reelected 2003, 2010, 2017

TIMELINE

IN RWANDA		IN THE WORLD
10,000 BCE		
Earliest settlements in Rwanda are established. The Twa hunt and gather.		**753 BCE** Rome is founded.
		116–117 CE The Roman Empire reaches its greatest extent under Emperor Trajan (98–117 CE).
		600 The height of the Maya civilization is reached.
		1000 The Chinese perfect gunpowder and begin to use it in warfare.
15th century Tutsi leader Ruganzu Bwimba establishes a kingdom near Kigali.		**1530** The beginning of the transatlantic slave trade is organized by the Portuguese in Africa.
		1558–1603 The reign of Elizabeth I of England takes place.
		1620 Pilgrims sail the *Mayflower* to America.
		1776 The U.S. Declaration of Independence is written.
		1789–1799 The French Revolution occurs.
19th century Kigeri Rwabugiri expands kingdom to its present borders.		**1861** The American Civil War begins.
1885 The Berlin Conference—Germany claims Ruanda-Urundi as part of German East Africa.		
1890s Europeans begin to arrive.		
1911–1912 German troops help the Tutsi incorporate Hutu regions into Rwanda.		
1914–1918 Belgium takes control of Rwanda.		**1914** World War I begins.
1923 League of Nations creates Ruanda-Urundi as a League Mandate to be ruled by Belgium.		**1939** World War II begins.

IN RWANDA	IN THE WORLD
1950s	
Belgians switch their support from the still-powerful Tutsi minority to the Hutu majority.	**1957** The Russians launch *Sputnik 1*.
1962 Rwanda becomes an independent republic. Grégoire Kayibanda is elected president	**1966–1969** The Chinese Cultural Revolution occurs.
1973 Major General Juvénal Habyarimana overthrows Kayibanda in a military coup and seizes power.	**1986** A nuclear power disaster occurs at Chernobyl in Ukraine.
1990 Rwandan Patriotic Front (RPF) launches invasion.	**1991** The breakup of the Soviet Union occurs.
1993 The Arusha agreement is signed.	
1994 Civil war and genocide erupt on April 7. The RPF invades on July 4. On July 18, cease-fire is declared. Pasteur Bizimungu is elected president.	**1997** Hong Kong is returned to China.
2000 In March, Bizimungu resigns; Paul Kagame is sworn in as president.	**2001** Terrorists crash planes in New York, Washington, D.C., and Pennsylvania on September 11.
2002 Gacaca courts are launched to try genocide perpetrators.	
2003 Paul Kagame is reelected.	**2003** The Iraq War begins.
	2008 Barack Obama is elected the first African American president of the United States.
2009 Rwanda joins the Commonwealth.	
2010 Paul Kagame is reelected for second 7-year term.	**2011** The Iraq War ends.
2012 The Rwandan Defense Force invades the Democratic Republic of the Congo.	
2017 Paul Kagame is reelected for a third 7-year term.	**2015** Over 80 nations sign the Paris Climate Agreement.
2020 Strict COVID-19 preventative measures are activated.	**2019** The COVID-19 outbreak begins in Wuhan Province, China.

GLOSSARY

abiiru
A small group of advisors who kept the Tutsi king accountable in ancient Rwanda.

bazimu
A spirit of the dead.

gacaca
A tribal judicial system.

igisoro
A game played by two people with a pitted board and seeds.

ikuma
A lance.

imigongo
Decorative tiles made from cow dung, ash, and clay.

ingabo
A shield.

intore
A special Rwandan dance troupe whose name means "the chosen one."

inzu
A family, household, or house.

isinde
A wicker jacket.

lulunga
A harplike instrument with eight strings.

mancala
A two-person game of strategy.

mushanana
A traditional garment made of one large cut of fabric.

mwami
A Tutsi king.

rugo
A traditional homestead.

tambourinaires
Drummers.

ubuhake
A form of feudalism in early Rwanda.

umeheto
A bow.

umuganda
A principle of community service.

umuryango
A patrilineal kinship unit.

FOR FURTHER INFORMATION

BOOKS

Fossey, Dian. *Gorillas in the Mist*. London, UK: Orion Publishing Group, 2001.

Gourevitch, Philip. *We Wish to Inform you That Tomorrow We Will Be Killed with Our Families: Stories from Rwanda*. New York, NY: Picador, 1999.

Hatzfeld, Jean, and Joshua David Jordan. *Blood Papa: Rwanda's New Generation*. New York, NY: Farrar, Straus and Giroux, 2018.

Sinalo, Caroline. *Rwanda After Genocide: Gender, Identity, and Post-Traumatic Growth*. Cambridge, UK: Cambridge University Press, 2018.

Thompson, Susan. *Rwanda: From Genocide to Precarious Peace*. New Haven, CT: Yale University Press, 2018.

WEBSITES

BBC News. "Rwanda Profile." www.bbc.com/news/world-africa-14093322.

CIA. *The World Factbook*. "Rwanda." www.cia.gov/the-world-factbook/countries/rwanda/.

Encyclopedia Britannica. "Rwanda." www.britannica.com/place/Rwanda.

The Government of the Republic of Rwanda. www.gov.rw/about.

World Culture Encyclopedia. "Rwanda." www.everyculture.com/No-Sa/Rwanda.html.

VIDEOS

Dian Fossey: Secrets in the Mist. Twentieth Century Fox Home Entertainment, 2017.

Rwanda: The Royal Tour. PBS, 2018.

The Uncondemned. Virgil Films, 2019.

BIBLIOGRAPHY

Azeda, Hope. "Can Art Heal a Broken Society?" *TIME*, October 24, 2018. time.com/5426864/rwanda-art-resilience/.

CIA. *The World Factbook*. "Rwanda." www.cia.gov/the-world-factbook/countries/rwanda/.

Halsey Carr, Rosamond, and Ann Howard Halsey. *Land of a Thousand Hills*. New York, NY: Viking, 1999.

Lemarchand, René, and Daniel Clay. "Rwanda." *Encyclopaedia Britannica*, February 26, 2020. www.britannica.com/place/Rwanda.

Moran, Benedict. "Rwanda's War Nearly Destroyed This Park. Now It's Coming Back." *National Geographic*, May 7, 2019. www.nationalgeographic.com/environment/2019/05/akagera-national-park-rwanda-conservation/#close.

Sinalo, Caroline. *Rwanda After Genocide: Gender, Identity, and Post-Traumatic Growth*. Cambridge, UK: Cambridge University Press, 2018.

Ssuuna, Ignatius. "Rwanda: Catholic Bishops Apologize for Role in Genocide." AP News, November 21, 2016. apnews.com/article/842d2a4f306c43f096a57039c2071fbe.

Uwiringiyimana, Clement. "Now Grown Up: The Rwandan Genocide Orphans Who Found a Bigger Family." Reuters, April 4, 2019. www.reuters.com/article/us-rwanda-genocide-families/now-grown-up-the-rwandan-genocide-orphans-who-found-a-bigger-family-idUSKCN1RG1D5.

Warton School. "Reinventing Rwanda: A Conversation with President Paul Kagame." October 22, 2015. knowledge.wharton.upenn.edu/article/president-paul-kagame-on-rwandas-reinvention/.

Wiafe-Amoako, Francis. *Africa*. Lanham, MD: Rowman & Littlefield, 2018.

INDEX

INDEX